CUSTOMS UNIONS AND TRADE CONFLICTS
The Enlargement of the European Community

CUSTOMS UNIONS AND TRADE CONFLICTS

The Enlargement of the European Community

G.N. Yannopoulos

ROUTLEDGE
London and New York

First published in 1988 by
Routledge
11 New Fetter Lane, London EC4P 4EE

Published in the USA by
Routledge
in association with Routledge, Chapman & Hall, Inc.
29 West 35th Street, New York NY 10001

Printed in Great Britain
by Billing & Sons Limited, Worcester.

British Library Cataloguing in Publication Data

Yannopoulos, George N.
    Customs unions and trade conflicts: the
    enlargement of the European Community.
    1. European Economic Community 2. Commerce
    I. Title
    382   HF1008
    ISBN 0-415-00389-X

Library of Congress Cataloging-in-Publication Data

Yannopoulos, George N., 1936–
    Customs unions and trade conflicts: the enlargement of the
European Community/G.N. Yannopoulos.
        p. cm.
    Author's papers originally presented at various international
conferences during the period 1981–87.
    Bibliography: p.
    Includes index.
    ISBN 0-415-00389-X
    1. European Economic Community countries — Commercial policy.
2. European Economic Community. 3. Customs unions. I. Title.
HF1532.92.Y36 1988
382.9'142 — dc 19   87-31038

CONTENTS

i

iii

LIST OF TABLES

LIST OF ABBREVIATIONS

ACP	=	African, Caribbean and Pacific states signatories of the Lomé convention
BRITE	=	Basic Research in Industrial Technology for Europe
CAP	=	Common Agricultural Policy
CET	=	Common External (or Customs) Tariff
CMEA	=	Council of Mutual Economic Assistance (COMECON)
CPEs	=	Centrally Planned Economies
DMEs	=	Developed Market Economies
EC	=	European Community
ECLA	=	United Nations Economic Committee for Latin America
ECSC	=	European Coal and Steel Community
ECU	=	European Currency Unit
EFTA	=	European Free Trade Association
ESPRIT	=	European Strategic Programme for Research and Developments in Information Technology
EUA	=	European Unit of Account
EUROSTAT	=	European Statistical Office
FAO	=	Food and Agricultural Organisation of the United States
GATT	=	General Agreement of Tariffs and Trade
GDP	=	Gross Domestic Product
GMP	=	Global Mediterranean Policy
GSP	=	Generalised System of Preferences
IMPs	=	Integrated Mediterranean Programmes
LDCs	=	Less Developed Countries
LLDCs	=	Least Developed Countries
MFA	=	Multifibre Arrangement
MFN	=	Most Favoured Nation clause
MTN	=	Multilateral Trade Negotiations
NCMC	=	Non-Candidate Mediterranean Countries
NICs	=	Newly Industrialising Countries
NTBs	=	Non-Tariff Barriers to trade
OECD	=	Organisation for Economic Cooperation and Development
PSOE	=	Spanish Socialist party
RACE	=	Research and Development in Advanced Communications Technology for Europe
R & D	=	Research and Development
SITC	=	Standard International Trade Classification
STABEX	=	Stabilisation of Export Earnings
VERs	=	Voluntary Export Restraints

PREFACE

This volume brings toghether several studies that examine the international trade ramifications of the geographical expansion of the European Community (EC). The focus of these empirical studies is primarily the enlargement of the EC during the 1980s. However, comparisons with the international trade implications of the first enlargement of the EC in 1973 are also reported.

The chapters of the book are fairly independent of each other but are linked together by a common theme : each examines a selected aspect of the trade impact of the enlargement of the EC on the rest of the world.

Most of the empirical studies included in this volume were published previously in professional journals, but some revisions were made to the original papers. I would like to thank the editors of the journals where the various chapters were originally published for their most generous assistance in permitting the idea of a volume on this important aspect of the international trade relations of the EC to become a reality. In particular, chapters 1 and 7 were originally published in the *Journal of World Trade Law* - the first in volume 19 and the second in volume 21. Chapter 2 appeared first in volume 28 of the *ACES (Association of Comparative Economic Studies) Bulletin*. The editors of the *Journal of European Integration* authorised the reprint of the article which was originally published in volume 4 of their journal and now appears as chapter 3 of this book. Chapter 4 is reprinted from *Development Policy Review*, volume 1. It is used by permission of Sage Publications Ltd., London. Copyright 1983 Overseas Development Institute, London. Chapter 5 first appeared in *World Development*, volume 12, published by Pergamon Journals Ltd, Oxford, UK. Chapter 6 was published originally in *Applied Economics*, volume 19. The last chapter of this volume appeared first in *Cahiers de Bruges*, N.S. 44 which included the proceedings of a conference organised by the College of Europe in July 1985 and edited by C. Cosgrove and J. Jamar under the title 'The European Community's Development Policy: the Strategies Ahead'.

All the papers included in this volume were presented at international conferences during the period 1981-87 organised by the European University Institute at Florence, the College of Europe at Bruges, the University of Naples, Italy, the Centre for European Studies of the City University of New York, the Hebrew University at Jerusalem, the University of Valencia, Spain, the Development Studies Association of the UK and the University Association of Contemporary European Studies (UK). To the organisers of these conferences I express my gratitude for the opportunities they gave me to receive helpful comments and criticisms of earlier drafts.

Finally I should like to thank Mrs. P. Elgar, the Departmental Secretary, who responded to the challenge of modern printing technology with unflagging enthusiasm and remarkable efficiency.

G.N. Yannopoulos

INTRODUCTION

1 The Issues

Both theory and practice suggest that neither the formation nor the geographical extension of customs unions lead necessarily to freer world trade. It is worth recalling that a staunch supporter of the German *Zollverein* - an early European experiment in customs unions - was the crusader of German protectionism, Friedrich List, precisely because he saw its formation as an instrument of protecting German industry from the pressures of British competition (Machlup, 1977). It is then not surprising to find that a number of contemporary writers on the economics of integration like Cooper and Massell (1965), Harry Johnson (1965) and Peter Robson (1984) argue that the most plausible rationale for the formation of customs unions is that they enable groups of countries to achieve more economically the objectives served by protectionism.

It can additionally be argued that on institutional grounds the geographical extension of established customs unions is in most cases likely to take place under circumstances encouraging a drift towards protectionism. Established customs unions are bound to yield effectively stronger bargaining power vis-a-vis their enlargement partners and for this reason they are not likely to be tariff averaging customs unions. At the same time the cumbersome decision making procedures that often characterise the institutions entrusted with the management of customs unions (unanimity or strongly qualified majority rules etc.) lead in such negotiations to the acceptance of the lower common denominator which in this instance is the position of the most protectionist government within the established customs union. Moreover when the customs union to be enlarged practises in its external commercial relations a system of multiple trade discrimination - as is the case with the European Community - then its geographical extension can easily give rise to a multitude of complicated trade conflicts with the rest of the world. As so many of the trade conflicts that have arisen or are arising from the past and present geographical extension of the European customs union are directly resulting from the discriminatory nature of the network of external commercial relations maintained by the European Community (EC) it is important at the outset to sketch briefly this multiple trade discrimination system.

2 The Hierarchy of Trade Policies

At the bottom of the EC's hierarchy of trade preferences are countries with which the Community trades on a simple Most Favoured Nation

1

basis. Two groups of countries are included in this category of the EC's least preferred trading partners: the developed market economies of non-Europe OECD and the centrally planned economies. But even within these groups special trading arrangements involving some form of preferential treatment can be found. New Zealand dairy products get special treatment subject to quantitative restrictions. The EC has concluded since 1977 two principal treaties on fisheries with the United States. Even within the socialist bloc of the centrally planned economies, the German Democratic Republic is treated differentially from the rest of the CMEA countries by having its trade classified as 'internal' German trade whilst Romania and Cuba are included among the recipients of the Generalised System of Preferences. Moreover, in the case of textiles and clothing the outwards processing arrangements existing between a number of the socialist countries of Eastern Europe and the EC give the former better market access conditions to the Community than those available to developing countries' exporters constrained by the Multifibre Arrangement.

At the apex of the EC's hierarchy of trade policies one finds two groups of countries : the 66 African, Caribbean and Pacific countries (ACP) of the Lomé Convention (now in its third five-year term) and the developed market economies of EFTA. The countries of the Lomé Convention enjoy duty and quota free access for over 99 per cent of their exports. ACP exports of CAP products are subject to reduced rates of levies whilst sugar and beef and a few other products are covered by special quota provisions. The EFTA countries maintain a free trade area in industrial products with the EC but their agricultural trade is excluded from preferential treatment and is governed by special agreements offering limited access. Cooperation has recently been extended to research and development by opening up EC research programmes like ESPRIT II, BRITE and RACE for participation by EFTA firms.

In the middle of the EC's pyramid of trading privileges are two groupings of countries : the non-ACP developing countries and the countries around the Mediterranean basin. The non-ACP developing countries - a group that includes the major countries of the Third World in Asia and Latin America - are offered a Generalised System of Preferences (GSP) from which Taiwan is however excluded. The duty free access provisions of the Community's GSP are subject to strict eligibility conditions, cover mainly non-agricultural products and are restricted by quota and other limitations. In fact, only about 10 per cent of the quota-controlled imports under the GSP are given tariff-free treatment (Hine, 1985). The countries of the Mediterranean region (with the exception of Albania and Libya) maintain with the EC a mosaic of preferential trading arrangements some of which are

2

association agreements envisaging the eventual establishment of a customs union (cases of Turkey, Cyprus, Malta and, before its accession to the EC of Greece), or a free trade area (cases of Israel and, before its accession to the EC, Portugal) and others are preferential trade and development cooperation agreements (cases of the Maghreb and Mashrek countries and, since 1980, of Yugoslavia). A simple trade preference agreement with Spain was in force from 1970 till the country's accession to the EC. The special features of the agreements of the Mediterranean policy of the EC are too complex to be described in a brief survey but the most important ones are discussed in subsequent chapters (see also Tovias, 1977).

Table 0.1: Distribution of Agricultural and Food Imports by Trade Policy Instrument Applied.

	Percentage of imports subject to:		
Countries of origin	Variable Customs Levies	Duties simple or in combination with counter-vailing charges	Zero Customs Duties
DMEs	12.6	34.2	53.2
CPEs	17.6	25.5	56.9
LDCs	9.4	34.2	56.4
of which			
ACP	(4.5)	(0.1)	(95.4)
Mediterranean	(5.9)	(69.1)	(25.0)
World	11.3	33.8	54.9

Source : Commission of the EC. Perspectives for the Common Agricultural Policy COM (85) 333 final, 13 July 1985.

The increasing use of VERs by the EC has led to the conclusion of a number of agreements regulating several exports to the Community. Such VERs are practised both towards developed and developing countries and cover a variety of products from motor cars and electronics to sheep and lamb meat. The growth of the clothing exports from the developing countries to the EC is regulated by the Multifibre Arrangement. Finally, for agricultural trade the Community operates in effect two parallel hierarchical arrangements with a product based hierarchy of import policy instruments coexisting with the country based hierarchy of preferences (Harris, Swinbank and Wilkinson, 1984).

3

Table 0.1 overleaf shows the way different instruments of controlling market access are applied to the agricultural exports of five groups of countries.

3 Re-orientation of Trade Flows

Within this complex system of multiple trade discrimination any territorial expansion of the European customs union is bound to induce extensive adjustments and re-orientation in trade flows and to give rise to numerous international commercial conflicts of varying degrees of seriousness.

The European Community completed in the 1970s its first enlargement that extended its membership from six to nine with the addition of Denmark, Ireland and the United Kingdom. It is now going through the process of accommodating its second enlargement which started in January 1981 with the accession of Greece and continued with the entry of the two Iberian economies, Portugal and Spain, in January 1986. Already early predictions are made for a third enlargement despite the manifest reluctance of several member states to contemplate such a move before the consequences of the present enlargement are sorted out. This process of transition will take at least a decade. However, a third enlargement cannot be excluded as Turkey and possibly Cyprus may start any moment knocking at the Community's door and as a resurgence of Norwegian interest in Community membership is not beyond the realm of possibility.

The second enlargement has already produced a number of trade disputes and generated anxieties to both more and less privileged countries in the preference hierarchy of the European Community's external commercial policy even before the completion of the rather lengthy transition period envisaged in the three treaties of accession. The second enlargement of the European Community with the extension of the Common Agricultural Policy (CAP) to three countries with relatively large agricultural sectors will inevitably shrink the 'free' segment of the international market in agricultural products. At the same time, it disturbs the delicate balance of interests built in the European Community's system of preferential trading with the ACP countries, the Mediterranean region and the rest of the developing world. Such commercial frictions are not just a special feature of the second enlargement of the EC. During the first enlargement of the Community the trade interests of the United Kingdom partners' in EFTA and in the Commonwealth had to be accommodated within the new reality of an expanded EC operating a common commercial policy vis-a-vis the rest of the world. The compromise was to make the then common external commercial policy less common than before. A free

4

trade area in industrial products with the UK's partners in EFTA that did not accede to the EC moved these countries upwards in the hierarchy of the EC's trade relations eroding the preference margins of the associates of the EC in the Mediterranean and elsewhere. Special arrangements had to be worked for New Zealand lamb and butter and for Cyprus sherry and potatoes.

A number of Commonwealth states from Africa, the Caribbean and the Pacific were brought into the privileged club of the EC's associates which was previously dominated by the francophone countries of the Yaoundé convention. Other Commonwealth countries were finally reconciled to the less attractive status of a GSP beneficiary. The interests of the countries receiving preferences in the markets of the UK, Ireland and Denmark could not possibly be fully accommodated within the enlarged Community of nine members without upsetting the interests of established customs union partners and their privileged associates. The result was that although the first enlargement of the EC produced from the world viewpoint a net increase in trade and welfare, some countries experienced a strong diversionary effect on their exports. That is, their exports to the combined EC and EFTA were 'retarded' by reaching levels below those that would have been attained in the absence of the first enlargement. Estimates by Kreinin (1974) of the impact of the first enlargement on trade flows in semi-manufactures and manufactures show that this diversionary effect was equivalent to 22.4% of their total exports to the EC and EFTA combined for the developed economies of the Commonwealth and 37.4% for the developing Commonwealth countries that did not become parties to the Lomé convention. There were other losers too including the rest of the developing world, the centrally planned economies and the USA (plus a few other developed market economies). Exports of the USA to the combined markets of EC and EFTA were 'retarded' because of the first enlargement by approximately 22% or by about $2,000 million (at 1970 prices). However, even before the first enlargement, the negotiation of a number of association agreements involving reciprocal preferences with several Mediterranean countries created protracted disputes between the EC and the US with the latter claiming that such trading practices were not within the spirit of article 24 of the GATT (Kreinin, 1976). The experience of these years demonstrated the danger of undermining the basic fabric of the international trading system from initiatives to expand either the boundaries or the sphere of influence of the EC. Such initiatives increase the degree of relative discrimination against outsiders whilst they erode the margin of preference of insiders. It can easily be shown that the larger the share of intra-union imports in the total imports of the customs union, the more serious will be the degree of trade discrimination against outsiders for any given level of common customs tariffs. Enlargement is bound to expand that share and thus raise the rate of trade discrimination against third countries. Let us define the rate of trade discrimination against third country exporters to the EC as the difference between the tariff charged to that exporter and the "average" tariff charged on all imports to the customs union irrespective of whether they originate from outside or inside the customs union area. Thus if the customs tariff for product j is denoted by t_j^c, the share of imports from other partner countries by q_j^c and the share from third countries by $(1 - q_j^c)$ then the "average" tariff paid on imports of product j into the EC is

$$t_j^c (1 - q_j^c) + 0.q_j^c$$

and the rate of trade discrimination becomes :

$$t_j^c - t_j^c (1 - q_j^c) = t_j^c q_j^c$$

Thus since q_j^c increases with the geographical extension of the customs union the rate of trade discrimination against the remaining outsiders is expected to increase. In a similar way the associates of the customs union before its enlargement will experience an erosion of their preferences either through competition from the new full members of the customs union or because new members bring along new associates to the club of privileged trading partners of the customs union. In the case of the second enlargement of the EC the degree of erosion of the margin of preferences enjoyed by the developing countries in the markets of EC-9 can be calculated as shown on p.7.

The diversion of trade against third countries and the erosion of preference of the 'privileged' associates have not been the only sources of trade conflicts generated by the geographical extensions of the European customs union. Conflicts can also arise because new members may be forced to abandon their own pre-existing preferential (or more liberal) trading arrangements with countries that subsequently find themselves outside the group of the privileged trading partners of the enlarged customs union - as happened with several Commonwealth countries that lost their preferences in the UK market upon the latter's accession to the EC. Put in a different way, the process of tariff realignment that follows the geographical extension of a customs union may result in an increase in the tariffs of the new members whose previous customs duties on imports from the rest of the world were lower than the common customs tariff they have to adopt after membership of the customs union. Thus the threat of external trade destruction will add another source of trade conflicts.

Let us adopt the following notation for the shares of imports in the enlarged EC-12 and the tariff rates applicable before and after enlargement.

EC imports from	% share	tariff rate before enlargement	tariff rate after enlargement
EC-9	q	0	0
New member states	r	t_M	0
DMEs (Developed Market Economies)	s	t_C	t_C
LDCs (Developing Countries)	x	t_L	t_L

New member countries' imports from

EC-9	u	t_P	0
Other new member countries	v	t_A	0
DMEs	w	t_A	t_C
LDCs	z	t_A	t_L

By definition : $q+r+s+x+u+v+w+z = 1$
It is assumed that $t_A > t_C$, $t_A > t_L$ and $t_C > t_L$.

For any product, say j, the preference granted to a given country can be defined as the difference between what the *average* importer pays and what that country pays.

Before enlargement all importers into the 12 countries pay for any given product on the average
$$0.q + t_M r + t_C s + t_L x + t_P u + t_A v + t_A w + t_A z \qquad (1)$$
The developing countries were facing an average tariff of
$$t_L x + t_A z \qquad (2)$$
So their rate of preference was the difference between (1) and (2), i.e.,
$$t_M r + t_C s + t_P u + t_A v + t_A w \qquad (3)$$
After enlargement, all importers of a given product to the 12 countries will pay on the average
$$0.q + 0.r + t_C s + t_L x + 0.u + 0.v + t_C w + t_L z \qquad (4)$$
The developing countries will be paying now a tariff of
$$t_L x + t_L z = t_L (x + z) \qquad (5)$$
So their rate of preference will be the difference between (4) and (5), i.e.
$$t_C s + t_C w \qquad (6)$$
The rate of preference after enlargement will be smaller than before

enlargement since $t_Cw < t_Mr + t_pu + t_Av + t_Aw$. The difference between these two expressions measures the rate of preference erosion.

4 Institutional Changes

It is obvious that the extent and direction of the required adjustments in trade flows from the geographical extension of a customs union will depend, *inter alia*, on the changes in the institutional setting governing the trade of the established customs union and the new members between them and with the rest of the world. For an understanding of the trade effects of the second enlargement, it is therefore important to specify clearly the institutional changes in the commercial relations between the three new members and the EC on the one hand and between them and the rest of the world on the other. The main changes in the trading regime of the three new members are briefly summarised in what follows. More details are given in the subsequent chapters of this volume. Greece's trading links before its accession to the EC were governed by the 1961 Greece-EC Association Agreement which provided for free trade in industrial products and considerable concessions on agricultural products. EC tariffs on Greece's exports of manufactures had been completely eliminated well before the 1979 Accession Treaty with the exception of textiles which were subjected to quantitative restrictions. On the other hand, Greek tariffs on EC exports have not been fully eliminated. Portugal's trade with the EC was governed by an Agreement dating back to 1972. This Agreement provided for free trade in industrial products and preferential treatment of Portuguese exports of agricultural products to the EC. On the basis of the 1972 Agreement all EC tariffs on Portugal's exports of manufactures had been removed well before the country applied for Community membership with the exception of Portuguese exports of textile products which were under a surveillance system. Portuguese tariffs on EC exports were only partially eliminated when the country signed the Treaty of Accession of 12 June 1985. Spanish-EC trade relations were governed by the 1970 Preferential Agreement which offered partial tariff reductions in industrial products from both sides with the EC conceding larger reductions than Spain. For most industrial goods the EC tariff reduction was equivalent to 60% of the common customs tariffs whilst the Spanish reduction was 25% of the national tariff. For a variety of manufacturing products (certain foodstuffs, cork and cork products, certain textile fibres and coal and steel products) no EC tariff reductions were envisaged whilst raisins, some cotton fabrics and refined petroleum products were offered preferential tariff quotas. Spain too maintained a list of manufacturing products (paper, electrical machines and appliances, fertilisers, plastics, steel etc.) for which no tariff reductions for EC exports were applicable. Regarding agricultural trade, partial tariff preferences were applicable on both sides (30% to 50% by the EC and up to 60% by Spain) but on the average around 35% of Spanish agricultural exports were not included in the preferential trading arrangements.

The post-enlargement trading regime will involve a complex set of changes in the external commercial links of the three new members with the EC and with the rest of the world. This new trading regime will take its final shape when the transition period is completed. The negotiated transition periods vary. For Greece, the transition period ends 1986/1988, according to products. For Spain and Portugal, the transition period extends up to 1 January 1993 for the provisions regarding free trade in industrial products and up to 1 January 1996 for agricultural products with earlier dates for beef and veal and fish products (1 January 1993). The Accession Treaties for the three new members are progressively introducing a new trading regime characterised by the following:

(i)   free trade in manufacturing goods between the three new members and the EC-9,

(ii)   free trade in agricultural products between the new member states and the EC-9,

(iii)   adoption of the Common Agriculture Policy and the associated trade policy instruments (export restitution, levies, calendar restrictions, reference prices, etc.),

(iv)   adoption of the EC's agreement with the EFTA countries involving free trade in industrial products and limited concessions in agricultural products; this applies to Greece and Spain only as Portugal was already a member of EFTA,

(v)   free trade in both manufactures and agricultural products between Greece and Spain, Greece and Portugal and Spain and Portugal,

(vi)   accession of all three countries to the EC's Generalised System of Preferences,

(vii)   participation by all countries in the third Lomé convention,

(viii)   adoption by the three new members of all individual agreements between the EC and the countries of the Global Mediterranean Policy,

(ix)   adoption of the EC restrictive agreements (voluntary export restraints, tariff quotas etc.) on textiles and other products (e.g. manioc, lamb, etc.) with a number of third countries,

(x)   withdrawal by both Greece and Spain from the 1971 Protocol of trade negotiations among developing countries which provides for reciprocal tariff preferences on a bilateral basis among its signatories.

The institutional changes brought about by the enlargement imply complex patterns of trade adjustments and are a potential source of trade conflicts some of which are likely to injure powerful actors that may result in retaliatory measures with uncertain consequences for the world trading system. Thus both from the point of view of the theory of international trade policy and the practice of international relations the second enlargement of the European Community raises vital questions. In order to address ourselves to these questions it is important to be able to indicate the kind and the size of the trade adjustments expected from the aforementioned institutional changes. This requires the adoption of a methodology to study ex-ante the effects of the enlargement of the EC on trade flows.

5 Methodological Questions

Absence of reliable estimates of price elasticities and of other variables required for the use of **direct** analytical methods forces us to rely on an **indirect** method of approximating the expected integration effects on trade flows. The ex-ante analysis used in this book builds upon the work of Balassa (1965), Kreinin (1974) and Donges et al (1982). The essence of the indirect method used in the case studies reported in this volume is to approximate the trade effects of the geographical extension of the customs unions on third countries through a step by step approach. The first step is to assess the quantitative importance of the overlap between the exports of the third countries and of the three new member states to the EC. This information is used to identify the sectors most exposed to export trade diversion.

The second step is to assess the revealed comparative advantage of a number of third countries in the markets of the EC and compare its recent trend with that of the three new member countries. In this exercise changes in the apparent penetration of exports into the EC markets are separately examined according to the degree of preference each regional group enjoys in the Community. Taken together, these two steps enable us to identify the vulnerable exports of third countries, i.e. to assess the extent of possible EC import trade diversion against third countries' exports.

Product supply responses are vital in determining whether any potential trade diversion will eventually materialise into actual trade displacement. This is why in the third stage of the indirect method used in the case studies reported in this volume an assessment is made of the supply potential and the supply response to expected changes in product price levels and costs in the new member states.

10

In this way we progressively built up the information required to judge the extent of (a) any trade diversion in favour of the new member states and against third countries and (b) any trade creation between the new members and third countries. Details of the particular techniques used in each of the stages of the indirect method described above are given in the individual chapters of this volume.

Whenever applicable the ex-ante evaluation is complemented by an ex-post analysis of the effects of the enlargement of the EC. This is particularly applicable to the effects of the first enlargement. The choice of the appropriate ex-post method is not an easy task.

In tracing the impact of the formation of customs unions on trade flows it is vital on the one hand to pose correctly the counter-factual (no-integration) situation and on the other to isolate successfully the integration effects from other contemporaneous factors, unrelated to the integration process, affecting trade flows. This last task can be undertaken by properly modelling the determinants of bilateral trade flows in the framework of an econometric model. The Tinbergen-Linemann gravity type of bilateral trade modelling has been used by Aitken (1973) and others in order to isolate the effects of intra-union tariff preferences from other influences on trade flows.

Less demanding - in data and effort - alternatives have been suggested by several authors including Balassa (1967), Kreinin (1972), Truman (1969) and Young (1972) (reviewed in Robson, 1984 and Mayes, 1978). Balassa offered the ex-post income elasticity of import demand method based on the assumption that in the absence of integration this elasticity would have stayed constant. Observing how this elasticity changes in both intra- and extra-area imports one is then able to establish the extent to which trade creation, trade diversion or net external trade creation have taken place. The application of this method to the case of the European customs union is subject to several difficulties such as integration induced changes in relative prices and exchange rates etc. (Sellekaerts, 1973).

Truman suggested the use of shares in apparent consumption as a convenient way of tracing the integration induced effects on trade flows. His suggestion is more within the spirit of the customs union theory since it takes explicitly into account changes in both production and trade flows. Kreinin (1972) has suggested the use of a third country as a 'normaliser' in posing the counter-factual situation. Young (1972) has also proposed the use of a 'control' group. By observing the evolution of the trade flows of the customs union members and the 'control' group of countries simultaneously in both the customs union market and in third markets one is able to isolate the

11

effect of income growth and autonomous changes in competitiveness thereby linking any impact of the customs union preference to the 'residual' remaining after this standardisation. The drawback with this approach is that its results depend very much on the choice of the countries to be included in the 'control' group; these countries must be distinguished by being treated differently from the reference countries in the EC markets but at the same time they must be characterised by similar supply capabilities as the group of reference countries.

The application of both ex-ante and ex-post methods to the analysis of available trade data yields strong indications of the possible redirection of trade flows that the second enlargement of the EC will bring about and enables us to isolate potential gainers and losers. The identification of the emerging trade conflicts is an important prerequisite in the design of the appropriate policy options to tackle them. The range of alternative policy options open to the EC and the international community in general are presented in the subsequent chapters within the context of the issues discussed in each separate case.

6 Plan of the book

The book starts with an analysis of the rationale and the structure of the common commercial policy of the European Community. This is an essential introduction to the understanding of the issues raised by the fact that the geographical extension of the European customs unions takes place within the specific framework of a particular common external commercial policy.

Chapters two to six present the major findings of the ex-ante studies estimating the effects on third countries of the recent geographical extension of the European customs unions. Chapter two looks at the impact of the enlargements of the EC on the trade of the centrally planned economies of the USSR and Eastern Europe. This chapter adopts a historical perspective and examines how East-West trade in Europe has been affected from the formation of the original customs union of the Six up to the recent second enlargement. The implications of the second enlargement for the trade interests of the developing countries are examined in chapters three and four. Chapter three looks at the global implications of the second enlargement on the Third World. Chapter four focuses on the consequences on the agricultural trade of the developing countries. Given the protective nature of the CAP the problems of agricultural trade certainly deserve special attention. The focus of chapter five shifts to the Mediterranean region - an area that has developed over the years special, preferential, trade links with the EC - and examines how its trade in manufactures is likely to be affected. Given the dominance of the Spanish economy in the group of the new members, chapter six looks in more detail on how Spain's accession will affect the trade interests (both in agricultural goods and in manufactures) of its main competitors and its main suppliers outside the EC. Chapter seven examines the sources and the implications of the additional trade conflicts that the new geographical extension of the European customs union has generated with the United States. The Iberian enlargement has generated fears among the EC Mediterranean regions particularly because of the agricultural supply potential of Spain. To alleviate these fears, a package of 'adjustment' measures has been introduced known as the Integrated Mediterranean Programmes. Chapter eight examines the external trade effects of these programmes and asks how far the adjustments spearheaded by these programmes generate complementarities or conflict with the non-member Mediterranean countries.

The book closes with a chapter exploring the trade options open to the EC in the new round of multilateral trade negotiations. Given the trade conflicts produced by the enlargement of the EC, does the new round of multilateral trade negotiations provide an opportunity for sorting out some of the thorny problems created? The last chapter provides an answer to this question by suggesting the basic features of an agenda for the Uruguay round of multilateral trade negotiations which will result in action to eliminate the source of trade conflicts discussed in this book. GATT multilateral negotiations have at least twice helped to defuse the trade tensions among industrialised countries generated by EC external commercial policies. The Kennedy round (and to a lesser extent the earlier Dillon round) reduced the trade discrimination effect of the formation of the original six-member European customs union whilst the Tokyo round played a similar role in relieving the trade discrimination effects of the first enlargement.

CHAPTER ONE

The European Community's Common External Commercial Policy

1 Introduction

A common external commercial policy is an indispensable complement to a customs union. It is indeed for this reason that the Treaty of Rome has singled out this field of activity to make explicit provisions for a genuine common policy. This policy is meant to encompass not only the establishment of a common external tariff but also export credit policy, the use of various instruments for consultation or cooperation with third countries, tariff preferences, and even economic and industrial cooperation including technology transfer (Commission of the EC, 1978). Articles 110-116 of the Treaty of Rome set out the goals of a common external commercial policy and the procedures to be followed by member states for agreeing on such a policy. The initiative to formulate a common policy on external trade is left to the Commission of the European Community whilst its final approval rests with the Council of Ministers. Despite the importance of a common external commercial policy for the proper functioning of a customs union, the European Community (EC) has not yet managed to develop a coherent policy in its external economic relations. Real progress towards a common commercial policy has been painfully slow because of both the design of policy and the nature of Community institutions. This chapter examines the objectives, instruments and institutions of the Community's external commercial policy in an effort to trace the sources of friction and the causes of indecision that inhibit the development of a coherent and effective policy.

2 Conflicting Objectives

The common commercial policy has been designed in order to attain two broad objectives. The first is to ensure efficient international specialisation. The second to promote an open world trading system. These goals are not always compatible. Encouraging efficient international specialisation may not necessarily require a policy of free trade. Accepting the responsibility to contribute to the development of an open and non-discriminatory international trading system implies a commitment to liberal, free, trade policies (Wolf, 1983). Strains arising from the simultaneous pursuit of these two objectives have been increasing particularly in the last ten years or so as a consequence of a number of developments in the world economy.

14

The persistence of high levels of unemployment under inflationary conditions leads to the emphasis on real wage rigidities and to the advocacy of a policy of protection. It is feared that in the presence of real wage rigidities free trade could lead to a rise in unemployment and a decrease in welfare. However, the macroeconomic effects of commercial policy depend crucially on the manner in which import restrictions are combined with other government policies. Under flexible exchange rates and real wage rigidities the imposition of a tariff whose proceeds are distributed neutrally will still produce contractionary effects on employment and output except in the event of a Metzler paradox (Eichengreen, 1983). Only when tariff revenues are used to finance production subsidies can import restrictions have expansionary effects on employment and output, since in this case the increase in tariffs raises nominal wages by the same amount that the production subsidy increases producers' prices whilst leading to real exchange rate appreciation. Even in this case, increasing import restrictions is not an optimal policy. If real wage rigidity is the only distortion in the system, then the optimal policy is a wage subsidy financed through lump-sum taxation. The next best policy is not protection either but a production subsidy to all industries facing real wage rigidities. Protection remains an inferior policy because it is equivalent to a production subsidy exclusively on import substitutes financed from a tax on their consumers (Brecher, 1974). Real wage resistance is the result of political-institutional factors and its solution lies in political-institutional changes (Lal, 1979). Furthermore the evidence on real wage resistance for the Community as a whole does not appear to be strong (Britton, 1983).

The predominance of industries operating under increasing returns to scale has also been emphasised as establishing a case for deviations from free trade either at the level of individual member states or at the level of the Community as a whole. As protectionist measures based on the economies of scale argument and applicable at the Community level may provoke retaliation, it is often suggested that they are imposed as specific both in terms of industries and with reference to trading partners (Noelke and Taylor, 1982). In the presence of increasing returns stemming from external economies or economies of 'learning by doing' the optimal policy response is not protection but a domestic tax and subsidy policy to be phased out over time (Bardhan, 1970). It is worth also pointing out here that to the extent that there exist unexploited economies of scale on a European-wide level, the explanation is not a lack of protection but rather the presence of internal barriers to European trade. Thus lack of success in liberalising the internal market of the Community leads inevitably to protectionist pressures vis-a-vis the rest of the world.

15

Far more important for its consequences for commercial policy is the growing significance of intra-industry trade. When international trade in differentiated products takes place then 'optimum tariff' arguments have more general applicability than in the classical case of trade in homogeneous goods. In a world of differentiated products rival firms produce different brands of the good in question, each variety being produced under increasing returns. In this case tariff protection will yield results similar to the traditional 'optimum tariff' argument. The imposition of a tariff on a foreign firm selling differentiated products and thus faced with a downwards sloping demand curve in the domestic economy, will induce that firm to reduce its price so that the domestic consumer pays a price increase less than the tariff. Thus, the domestic economy gains by acquiring goods more cheaply (Kierzkowski, 1984). Provided that the increased profits of the domestic firms induce further entry into the industry then the overall effect is increased employment and a more efficient scale of production. When free entry conditions to the industry are not present and a zero profit equilibrium cannot be brought about then the gains from protection are captured as higher profits by domestic firms. Given the fact that the employment gains will still be forthcoming, the net welfare gain for small tariffs may still be positive for the economy. When intra-industry trade is present an 'optimum tariff' case can thus be made. The size of the welfare gain will depend on the price response of the foreign supplier and the elasticity of substitution between the local and the imported variety of the product. It can then be argued that the more extensive intra-industry trade becomes, the more justification governments will find to use 'optimum tariff' arguments in the shaping of their external commercial policies.

Apart from 'optimum tariff' pressures when trade consists of differentiated products, the strategic use of tariff to influence the outcome in industries where the locational equilibrium is indeterminate has also been advocated - especially in 'high technology' sectors and 'natural' oligopolies where the industries are highly concentrated at the level of the world economy and where economies of scale are considerably high (Shaked and Sutton, 1984). In these cases, the location of industry under free trade is not uniquely determined by international differences in factor prices but instead multiple equilibria exist (Sutton 1984). The emergence of new technologies not only increases the pressures for protectionist measures to distribute more evenly over time the resulting adjustment costs but also induces governments to use tariffs strategically to influence the world location pattern of the new 'high technology' industries.

The balance of payments constraint has also been suggested as a basis for advocating European-wide protectionist policies (Cripps, 1983).

If an individual Community country expands out of phase with the rest of Europe and runs a balance of payments deficit as a result, a loss of confidence in its currency may force that country into a disorderly devaluation. If the Community as a whole expands broadly at the same rate, this serious confidence problem is less likely to arise. A small adjustment to interest rates will probably be enough to manage the situation. Even if we assume that the balance of payments is actually the operative constraint on expansion for some countries, it does not follow that generalised protection is the best policy of maintaining confidence in the value of a currency. Protection of manufacturing production will not be enough to prevent a deterioration of the current account since for Europe as a whole imports of manufactures from the rest of the world account for less than 50 per cent of all imports from the rest of the world. Global, European-wide, protectionism does not provide an efficient balance of payments adjustment mechanism.

In summary, the Community finds it increasingly difficult to reconcile its objectives of maintaining free trade and in promoting an efficient pattern of international specialisation in a world dominated by intra-industry trade, "natural" oligopolies and market rigidities. Such conflicts in policy goals are bound to create confusion as to the direction the common external commercial policy is taking at times.

3 Inappropriate Instruments?

Leaving aside the problems raised from conflicts among the goals of the EC's common external commercial policy, it is also important to focus on the appropriateness of the instruments placed at the disposal of the Community institutions for pursuing these objectives. Here four types of problems have emerged:

(i) **The slow process of standardisation of import and export regulations** often places traders located in some member states at a more advantageous position vis-a-vis traders operating in other Community countries. Following the 1962 Common Commercial Policy Action Programme some progress was achieved in standardising import and export regulations, in harmonising export aids and in policies on anti-dumping. However in several cases harmonisation was achieved through external rather than Community initiatives. On export credits, it was the Arrangement negotiated in the OECD that brought about policy harmonisation in this area within the EC (Pearce, 1983). Furthermore, thanks to the fact that the Community is a party to the GATT Codes on Anti-dumping and Subsidies and Countervailing Duties, Community-wide standards and policies now exist in this field.

There are several areas where lack of harmonisation is noticeable. Despite the fact that the common external tariff has been operative since 1968, and despite the customs valuation code of the Tokyo Multilateral Trade Negotiations (MTN), lack of harmonisation of customs policy still persists. Community legislation covers only partly the provisions of the Kyoto convention (on the simplification and harmonisation of customs procedures) on issues like the temporary admission of goods for inward processing, the temporary exportation for outward processing, free zones (Commission of EC, 1984a) and the date of entry in the accounts of amounts of duty resulting from a customs debt (Commission of EC, 1985). The lack of a common customs policy has been vividly demonstrated by the "battle of Poitiers" incident when, in October 1982, France forced importers of Japanese video equipment to process them only through the provincial city of Poitiers and designated other cities as "harrassment havens" for products such as furs and art objects. It is only in the trade instruments of the CAP where progress towards the development of a common policy has been satisfactory - although towards the wrong direction.

(ii)   **A reluctance of member states to transfer trade policy instruments from the national to the Community institutions** is noticeable in several issues. Despite the fact that the Treaty of Rome required that all bilateral trade agreements should be coordinated by 1970, the situation is still far from satisfactory. A Council decision of 16 December 1969 set out procedures for the progressive standardisation of agreements concerning commercial relations between member states and third countries and on the negotiation of Community agreements. Despite the expiry of the transitional period member states still continue to ask for an extension or tacit renewal of bilateral trade agreements on the ground that these extensions or renewals are essential to avoid disruption of their commercial relations. Such extensions or renewals are given subject to the conditions that (a) they would neither constitute an obstacle to the opening up of Community negotiations with the third countries concerned and the subsequent transfer of the commercial substance to Community agreements and (b) they would not hinder the adoption of measures necessary to complete the standardisation of the import arrangements applied by member states. It is in the trade with Eastern European countries that these agreements proliferate but they are equally spotted in trade with other Western European partners (Commission of EC, 1984b). In case of renewal of agreements consultation procedures with the Commission and other member states are normally adhered to; but this hardly constitutes a common policy. Bilateral agreements in shipping services between EC member states

18

and third countries have also spread widely raising concern not only by Community institutions but also by governments of member states (Commission of EC, 1984c).

The competence of the Community institutions to carry out an investigation before safeguard or surveillance measures are adopted was established only in 1982 (Gard and Riedel, 1981). The regulation of February 1982 sets out criteria for determining the extent to which the harm (actual or potential) is serious enough to warrant the introduction of safeguard measures. Before 1982 safeguard actions were also introduced unilaterally by a member country. Although the approval of the Community institutions was subsequently sought in most cases it amounted to presenting them with a fait accompli. However, it is only as from 1985 that member states are obliged to ask in advance the agreement of the Commission before they take safeguard actions. It is apparent that in order to avoid trade deflection safeguard actions must be implemented on a Community-wide basis even if they involve restrictions limited to a single country. The authority to grant safeguard relief depends however on whether the offending imports are included in the list of 'liberalised' products to which the CET applies. If this is the case, then the safeguard relief must be decided by the Community institutions. In other cases, safeguard action can be taken directly by member states subject to the provisions of the GATT (article XIX). Although protection in textiles and steel products takes place through channels other than the safeguard provisions (quotas limiting the import growth in the case of textiles and minimum import prices in the case of steel) nevertheless it is important to emphasise that here the common commercial policy appears to work effectively.

Voluntary Export Restraints (VERs) are measures where national actions can still be taken despite the attempts of the Commission to assume full responsibility on policy in this area. In consumer electronics both the UK, France and Italy operate agreements placing ceilings on the market share of various consumer electronics with Japan and other NICs. It has been estimated (Bondy, 1983) that the nations of the EC have concluded around 100 VERs with other countries. Yet, even in the case of vehicles where a mandate was given to the Commission by the Council to negotiate a VER with Japan member states proceeded almost at the same time to strike bilateral agreements with Japan. The reasons for the difficulties faced by the Community to agree on a common policy to combat disruptive influences of third countries' policies are discussed below (section 4).

(iii)   **A third problem has to do with the misdirection of the existing trade policy instruments.**

The commitment of the Community to an open world trading system has been repeatedly emphasised (Commission of EC, 1984d; European Economy, 1984). However, the use that the Community institutions make of the common policy instruments, particularly of the CET has drawn repeated criticisms by advocates of a liberal world trading order. The prohibitive nature of many of the trade instruments of the CAP has resulted in misallocation of world agricultural resources, enhanced the instability in world agricultural markets and added further disincentives to agricultural production in the less developed countries (LDCs). The attempt to meet the surge of imports from LDCs by turning the Multifibre Arrangement (MFA) into more or less a permanent institution of managed trade in textiles and clothing and by invoking frequently safeguard measures outside these sectors, has increased the insecurity of access to EC markets with adverse consequences on manufacturing growth in LDCs.

Even more serious because of its long-term consequences is the system of multiple trade discrimination that the Community evolved over the years. The network of EC agreements allowing for various degrees of preferential trade conflicts with the principles of the multilateral trade system developed under the auspices of the GATT, i.e. unconditional MFN treatment and non-discrimination. The regionalist approach followed by the EC in effect extends its preference system beyond the 100 per cent preference permitted under article 24 of GATT (Robertson, 1969). The non-discriminatory trade system involving strict reciprocity has thus been seriously eroded by the multi-tier preferential system developed by the EC, raising fears for more malign forms of discrimination like the system of 'new reciprocity' (Cline, 1983) which has crept into the US Trade and Tariff Act of 1984 (Patterson, 1984).

The system of discriminatory trade agreements generates political tension and friction between different countries and tends to shift the burden of adjustment to the third countries at the bottom of the EC's hierarchy of privilege. Moreover, as the possibilities of trade creation between the associated countries and the EC are limited, trade diversion against third developing countries with limited market access is likely to be relatively serious. Such a system cannot be regarded as always compatible with international commitments embodied in the GATT.

Disregarding for the moment the incompatibility of the regionalist approach pursued by the EC and the multilateral approach to international trade advocated by the GATT, we have to ask ourselves

20

how far this system is coherent and how far it really serves either the interests of the EC or the LDCs.

The system as it now stands represents an untidy collection of agreements, a piece-meal approach to trade matters. A comparison of the content of the various agreements signed within the so-called Global Mediterranean Policy illustrates this point well (Shlaim and Yannopoulos, 1976).

The system has not probably been conceived with a clear idea of its relevance for the interests of the EC. To refer again to the Mediterranean policy, it is by now clear that the development of this policy proceeded not on the basis of a well conceived design to safeguard the strategic and trade interests of the member states of the Community but essentially as a response to pressures placed on the Community by individual countries in the region that felt more heavily the trade discriminating effects from the formation of the EC (Tinbergen, 1960). Nor can the agreement with the ACP countries be said to safeguard vital interests of the member states of the EC. It can hardly be claimed that the ACP countries provide either energy supplies security (with the exception of uranium supplies) or fast growing outlets for the manufacturing exports of the Community. Both the major oil suppliers and the faster growing importers of manufactures are to be found outside the group of the EC's privileged partners. Even in the case of non-fuel minerals continued dependence on raw materials from the ACP States in the face of progressively declining European ownership of ACP mining industries and reduced rates of exploration and investment activities does not provide the best arrangement for supplies security (Daniel, 1984). It does not appear either that the Community is interested in taking advantage of what Hirschman called the influence effect of trade (Hirschman, 1945) and Marrese and Vanous (1983) unconventional gains from trade i.e. military, political, ideological or economic non-market benefits from bilateral preferential trade agreements; for, despite being an economic giant, the Community still is a political dwarf. Of course, it could still be the case that the building up of spheres of influence by means of preferential trade agreements may enable the Community exporters, as Roemer (1977) has suggested on another occasion, to market their weakest sectors of manufactures (i.e. sectors where their comparative advantage is weak) in the regions where their special trading links enable them to penetrate these markets easily. Channels of communication and information are more highly developed between countries in a sphere of influence relationship - a factor that reduces the costs of scanning the world markets to their importers.

21

On balance, it seems that the interests of the EEC might be better served by pursuing at least vis-a-vis the developing world a global policy in place of the present regionalist one. This move is politically difficult to make because of the resistance of associates to improved market access by outsiders but especially because a global policy by giving better access to outsiders will hurt producers inside the Community (Pinder, 1973). Given these difficulties, the alternative is a policy of rational differentiation and careful graduation.

The Community has already started building elements of this approach into the present system. The nine non-ACP least developed countries (LLDCs) have currently been provided with duty-free and tariff quota free access under the 1981 GSP system enjoying in this way a similar status to that of the LLDCs of the Lomé convention (Hewitt, 1982). Their access to the EC markets of agricultural goods was similarly harmonised with the exception of tobacco and instant coffee. The principle of graduation has been conceded in the 1981 GSP with the distinction between 'competitive' and 'non-competitive' LDCs made for the group of sensitive products. The basis of this distinction may not be sound (Wall, 1983) but what matters in this context is the introduction of a principle that may be more usefully extended to other areas of EC trade policy. Differentiation and graduation will ensure that the limited resources that the EC can transfer to the developing countries under the present economic climate are not diluted through the introduction of a global policy but instead are more effectively utilised.

(iv) The need for new commercial policy instruments

In a world of managed trade countries need to have appropriate policies to respond to the trade-distorting policies of other nations (Baldwin and Thompson, 1984). In a memorandum, prepared in 1982, France argued that the use of anti-dumping and safeguard measures cannot effectively tackle all unfair trading practices of other countries. It was pointed out, in particular, that the Community does not possess a trade policy instrument similar to that provided by section 301 of the US Trade Act 1974 and according to which the American President can suspend or withdraw trade agreement concessions or impose duties and other restrictions on the imports of offending countries. The Commission put before the Council in 1983 a proposal for a new commercial policy instrument which effectively consists of a mix of instruments and measures including speeding up the whole procedure for countermeasures to penalise unfair trade practices by third countries even in cases where they inflict injury to Community producers in third markets. A broad range of prejudicial practices are to be covered by the use of the new Community

22

commercial policy instruments. However, four member states including Britain have stated that they will be prepared to see this new commercial policy instrument used by the Commission only if a qualified majority of the Council approves of its decision to act.

Given the weaknesses of the dispute settlements procedure of the GATT (Jackson, 1978) a policy of appropriate unilateral trade retaliation is a more efficient way to deal with unfair trade practices (Goldstein and Krasner, 1984). Such an instrument when exercised with care may in practice elicit cooperation and freer trade rather than lead to trade wars. Cooperation is more likely under conditions of an iterative prisoners' dilemma, provided that both parties are quick to punish and quick to forgive (Axelrod, 1981).

4 The nature of Community institutions

The short excursion into the making and implementation of the Community's common external commercial policy clearly reveals the difficulties encountered in moving towards a comprehensive and coherent policy over the years. The nature of the Community institutions is of some importance here.

There is, first of all, the question of the competence of Community institutions in matters of external trade policy. This issue has surfaced both during the Tokyo MTN and, more recently, in the 1982 EC-US steel dispute. The Treaty of Rome provides that commercial agreements can be accepted on behalf of the EC, by a decision of the Council, upon the recommendation of the Commission. At the conclusion of the Tokyo MTN certain member states argued that the MTN agreements were mixed, rather than purely commercial ones, and consequently they should have been approved and signed both by the Community institutions and the governments of member states. As a compromise three of the agreements were characterised in this way (those concerning technical barriers to trade, aircraft and the tariff protocol) and were thus accepted additionally by member states (Jackson, 1983).

The question of competence has been raised especially during the period of the 'steel war' of summer 1982 because of a fundamental difference between the Rome and the Paris (ECSC) treaties (Benyon and Bourgeois, 1984). In the latter, it is explicitly mentioned (article 71) that in matters of commercial policy the powers of the member states that signed the ECSC Treaty are not affected. This is in contrast to article 113 of the Treaty of Rome and thus creates an anomaly that has to be sorted out at the expense of speedy decisions. In the

23

particular case of the steel dispute the confusing situation was sorted out by giving an extensive mandate to the Commission to negotiate an overall arrangement with the US government.

However, even when no mandate is required, the Commission still must obtain authorisation to commence negotiations. To reach a common position intensive internal bargaining needs to take place. This has a number of disadvantages. First, it allows the most protective member state to have the loudest voice. Compromises are usually struck at the lowest common denominator, which often means the most protective position. This tendency, is no doubt strengthened by the lack of internal, Community-wide, policies for industrial adjustment assistance. Secondly, in the process of a compromise commercial policy issues are often linked to internal policy issues; this leads eventually to the externalisation of the resulting conflicts and pressures with the result of shifting the common commercial policy towards interventionism. The common commercial policy eventually agreed has the characteristics of a political bargain, which makes policy positions rigid and inflexible and therefore difficult to adjust because of the reluctance to go again through the process of agreeing a new position. This can hinder international efforts for further trade liberalisation. Another consequence of all this is that the Community institutions are regarded as inflexible negotiators and dealings with them in international fora become both complex and time consuming. The new single European Act may contribute towards the removal of some of these rigidities.

Ultimately, the inability of the Community to resolve successfully internal conflicts, spreads eventually into the external trade policy field. The inability to rationalise steel production within the EC and to embark instead upon an extensive subsidisation programme led eventually to trade conflicts with the USA. Failure of the rest of the Community footwear industries to adjust to the strong competitive position of the Italian footwear sector leads to higher barriers on extra-Community trade. Managing disruptive outsiders becomes a softer option to managing disruptive insiders.

The result of all these institutional weaknesses is the lack of coherence in external trade policies. Lack of coherence leads often to measures of defensive interventionism. Defensive interventionism destabilises the trade policy environment. A manifestation of this is the protectionist leapfrogging game between the USA and the EC in industries like steel, textiles etc. (Wolf, 1983).

Perhaps because of the problems of decision-making within the EC in reaching trading positions, the Community has often been reluctant to use the trade disputes procedure of the GATT. The weakness of this procedure has been commented upon already. However, there is no evidence that the Community institutions have been taking an active part in improving the GATT dispute settlement process and in bringing a more effective self-enforcing framework of a quasi-judicial nature for settling trade conflicts among countries. Neither has the EC accepted the authority of the Textile Surveillance Board - a multilateral body with judicial functions - in matters relating to the implementation of the MFA. The Community has thus given so far the impression that it prefers "power diplomacy" rather than "rule diplomacy" in the settlement of international trade policy disputes. This may not be in the best interest of the Community. To illustrate this point one can refer again to the EC-US steel dispute of 1982. The vagueness and imprecision with which the Tokyo Round Subsidies Code defines the appropriate level of trade impact required to designate a subsidy as an offensive one allowed a unilateral US definition and the subsequent imposition of countervailing duties on iron and steel imports from the EC (Dominick, 1984). The nebulous compromise reached in the Tokyo Round on domestic subsidies leaves plenty of scope for the exercise of power diplomacy. But power diplomacy cannot work to the advantage of political dwarfs.

5 Trade Policy and Trade Performance

The tendency of the common external commercial policy of the EC to drift towards defensive interventionism and the preference for a regionalist approach in place of the multilateral approach of the GATT, have led many to fear that the outwards looking orientation of the European production system may be impaired through time. The trade performance of the Community does not justify these fears. The EC's industrial export ratio (proportion of industrial output exported) vis-a-vis the rest of the world is the highest of the industrialised countries. It stands (1980) at 18.4 per cent - i.e. more than three percentage points higher than that of Japan and more than twice as high as that of the US (8.9 per cent). The Community's industrial penetration ratio (ratio of extra-Community imports to industrial output) is at 13.8 per cent, 50 per cent higher than that of the USA and more than twice that of Japan. The Community's share of imports from LDCs to total imports increased from 18.1% in 1973 to 24.4% in 1981. The corresponding incremental ratio over the period 1973-81 was even higher (26.8 per cent). Even in import categories where the impact of 'new protectionism' has been strong, the record of openness of the Community compares favourably with both the USA and Japan (see table 1.2).

25

Thus whilst trade policy has been moving towards a protectionist stance, trade performance has shown signs of an increasing outwards orientation of the European economy. How can this be explained? The formation of the EC and its subsequent enlargement in 1973 has led to countermoves for multilateral tariff negotiations in an effort to reduce the trade discrimination effects of the Community's customs union.

Table 1.1: Relative importance for the EC of trade in manufactures with LDCs.

	1973	1981	1973-81
Share of imports from LDCs in total imports	18.1	24.4	-
Share of increment of imports from LDCs to increment of total imports	-	-	26.8

Source : B. Balassa (1984)

Table 1.2: Changes in Import Penetration Ratios, 1978-81
(percentage change of the imports/GDP ratio)

	EEC	USA	Japan
Total Imports			
Iron & Steel	-16	25	94
Passenger Vehicles	23	19	-33
Telecommunications Equipment	32	31	23
Imports from LDCs			
Textiles	-10	13	-32
Clothing	23	17	-4
Other Consumer Goods	36	40	3

Source: B. & C. Balassa (1984)

The Dillon Round but particularly the Kennedy and Tokyo Rounds of MTNs can be interpreted as attempts by the USA and the rest of the industrialised world to reduce the trade discriminating effects of the Common Market and its subsequent geographical extension. The result of these moves is that the average level of duties has fallen from 11% at the time of the introduction of the CET to 7.5% after the completion of the Tokyo Round reductions. Furthermore, it is argued that the acceptance of the GSP principle - despite earlier opposition - by the United States had much to do with the desire of the US to see the EC system of preferential trade with the LDCs dismantled. Thus, the presence of the Community as an important actor in world trade has led to the acceleration of the tariff dismantling process since the early 1960s. Unfortunately, it has not as yet produced similar catalytic effects in stemming the tide of 'new' protectionism.

CHAPTER TWO

The Impact of Western European Integration on East-West Trade

1 Introduction

The formation of a customs union disturbs established patterns of trade between the partners of a customs union and the rest of the world in a number of distinct ways. Initially (pre-integration) cheaper imports from non-partners may be replaced by expensive imports from a partner country; third countries may experience an expansion of their exports to the customs union if the external tariff rates of some partner countries were higher than the common external tariff adopted; in other cases third countries may see their trade with members of a customs union destroyed if the external tariff rates of the latter have to be raised to the higher level of the union common external tariff; the attraction of the markets of partner countries may induce other partners to shift part of their exports from third countries to the customs union area; finally, trade with third countries is bound to be affected by the actions taken by member countries to re-equilibrate payments following disturbances in their balance of payments as a result of the reorientation of trade induced by the formation of the customs union. Thus on the basis of the five possible developments just discussed one can conceptually distinguish five sources of integration-induced disturbances in the pattern of trade flows between a customs union and third countries; trade diversion, external trade creation, external trade destruction, supply-side diversion and balance of payments induced adjustments (El-Agraa, 1980a).

The relative size of each of these effects depends on the particular characteristics of the customs union in question. The incidence of these effects on particular third country suppliers will be influenced, among other things, by the composition of their exports to the customs union. In the case of the European Community customs union, the incidence of the various disturbances on trade flows with third countries will also depend on the position that a particular third country supplier has in the hierarchy of tariff preferences of the Community. The countries of the CMEA with the exception of Romania (which enjoys GSP status) and GDR (as far as its trade with W. Germany is concerned) occupy a position at the bottom of the EC's hierarchy of preferences and as such are likely to be more adversely affected by the negative effects of the disturbances on trade flows produced by the formation and enlargement of the European customs union.

28

It is the purpose of this chapter to look into the available empirical evidence in order to establish how far the net effect on Eastern European exports to the EC from the establishment and subsequent enlargements of the European customs union has been positive or negative. Supply side diversion effects and induced balance of payments adjustment effects are disregarded in what follows. The emphasis is placed on trade diversion and on external trade expansion and destruction.

2 Effects from the initial launching of the Community

A number of studies have been undertaken to trace the impact on EC imports from Eastern Europe following the launching of the Community by its six initial partners. Both Balassa (1975) and Sellekaerts (1971) have used the ex-post income elasticity of import demand to estimate what they called 'a Common Market effect' on Community imports from the CMEA area.

Under the assumption of a constant income elasticity of the demand for extra-area imports prior to and after the year the customs union was actually established it is possible to derive this 'Common Market effect' as the algebraic sum of two estimates of extra-area imports from a specific supplier: first, the hypothetical level of imports from that specific supplier (i.e. in our case the CMEA) during the period prior to the formation of the EC that would have resulted if the EC's imports from that specific supplier were evolving in the same way as its total imports from all extra-area suppliers to the EC and secondly, the hypothetical level of imports from the same specific supplier during a comparable post-integration period that would have resulted if imports (measured at constant prices) from that specific supplier were expanding (or contracting) at the actual average annual growth rate of the EC's extra-area imports from all suppliers. The choice of the initial period and the length of that period are obviously crucial; both starting and terminal years must correspond to similar phases of the business cycle to avoid biasing the results.

If the algebraic sum of these two estimates is positive then it indicates that the particular third country suppliers realised exports to the EC in excess of what would have been predicted on the basis of the performance of all extra area suppliers and without the formation of the European customs union. The 'Common Market effect' thus estimated is clearly separated from the competitive and the price effects on third country exports to the EC. The competitive effect can be measured as the difference between the value (in constant prices) of

29

imports at the terminal year of the post-integration period and the value of the hypothetical imports in the same year.

The 'Common Market effect' during the period the Community consisted of six members expressed as a percentage of the actual imports of the EC-6 from the CMEA countries is shown in table 2.1. For comparison purposes the corresponding figures for the relative importance of the Common Market effect for other groups of countries at the same position of the EC's preference hierarchy during the period are also given.

It is evident from these figures that the formation of the Common Market produced a net trade diversion effect when all CMEA exports to the EC are taken together. Only the group of 'other developed countries' has been inflicted with relatively heavier negative Common Market effects than the CMEA countries. This relatively higher impact of the net trade diversion effects is due primarily to the fact that the composition of the CMEA exports to the EC was not characterised by a heavy concentration in the products where external trade creation effects took place (machinery, transport, equipment, fuels). Furthermore, the relative size of the external trade creation effect on sectors like machinery or fuels was more modest in the case of the CMEA countries than in the case of the USA, the UK or Continental EFTA. This may have to do with the internal supply constraints in the Eastern European countries.

The composition of CMEA exports to the EC was not thus favourable in the sense that it did not concentrate particularly in sectors that profited from the external trade creating effects of the EC. In 1970, 51% of total exports consisted of chemicals, food products and other manufactures - sectors where the trade diversion effects of the EC were strong.

This is the case also when we go beyond the one-digit level of aggregation of table 2.1. Comparing ex-post income elasticities of import demand in the EC for agricultural products Thorbecke and Pagoulatos (1975) found evidence of external trade creation in extra-EC agricultural imports only in three out of 14 two-and-three digit SITC commodity groupings they examined, namely in feedstuffs (SITC 081), maize (SITC 044) and dairy products (SITC 022, 023, 024). External trade creation in feedstuffs and maize was accounted by the rapidly growing demand within the EC for meat, whilst in the case of dairy products it was related to significant increases in the demand for milk within the EC giving rise to a fourfold expansion of Community extra-area imports of milk between 1961-62 and 1968-69.

Table 2.1 : Common Market Effect as Percentage of 1970 Actual Exports (Valued in 1959 Prices)

Product Group	CMEA	USA	UK	Continental EFTA	Other developed countries	Non-Associated LDCs
Food, Beverages and Tobacco	-16.9	-18.1	-11.0	-33.5	-21.7	-23.5
Raw Materials	- 1.8	- 2.1	- 3.5	- 2.5	- 2.5	- 3.9
Fuels	+19.4	+40.0	+25.2	+26.9	+ 2.1	+16.8
Chemicals	-18.7	-14.2	-18.6	-17.6	- 8.6	-41.5
Machinery	+35.2	+48.7	+75.2	+73.7	+10.0	+ 9.4
Transport Equipment	+16.2	+17.0	+24.8	+13.6	+ 1.9	+21.1
Other Manufactures	-18.2	-15.9	-29.2	-27.6	-11.5	-26.6
All above	- 4.0	+ 5.1	+ 8.4	- 1.6	- 8.0	+ 0.3

Source: Calculated from data appearing in B. Balassa (ed.), *European Economic Integration*, North Holland Publishing Company, 1975, pp.393-398.

However, the group of these products with external trade creation effects are not of export interest to the CMEA.

Not all CMEA countries had equally gained from the external trade creating effects of the EC. CMEA countries with a commodity composition of their exports to the EC heavily weighted by products where the external trade creating effects of the EC were concentrated had benefited on balance from the creation of the Common Market. Estimates by Sellekaerts (1971) indicate that Bulgaria, the GDR, Hungary, Romania and Yugoslavia had been favourably affected by the formation of the EC i.e. the estimated external trade creation effect outweighed any adverse trade diversion effects.

3 The Proliferation of Community Preferences

The geographical extension of a customs union is bound to intensify the trade discriminating effects from the elimination of trade barriers between the initial customs union and its new partners. At the time of the first enlargement of the EC (i.e. the 1973 enlargement to include the UK, Denmark and Ireland) Kreinin (1973) estimated the net trade diverting effect against CMEA suppliers of manufacturing products to amount to 15.9 per cent of their total exports to the enlarged Community (EC-9) (Table 2.2). This estimate covers only semi-manufactures and finished manufactures and was derived by viewing the EC and EFTA (and their associated states) as two regions merging into one in the sphere of manufacturing goods. To compare the estimated impact of the first enlargement of the EC with the Common Market effect from the completion of the customs union of the original six members we calculated the relative size of the Common Market effect reported in table 2.1 separately for SITC groups 5,6,7 and 8. For these four SITC divisions the net trade diverting effect against CMEA suppliers amounted to 10.1 per cent.

The first enlargement of the EC marks also a period of proliferation of a variety of tariff preferences granted by the Community to several groups of countries. As these preferences were granted to non-CMEA countries the trade discriminating effects against CMEA suppliers have been further magnified. The group of EFTA countries provides a relevant 'control' group to judge the impact of these developments on CMEA exports to the enlarged EC. Prior to the first enlargement of the Community both EFTA and CMEA exporters were facing similar market access conditions to the EC markets. Following the enlargement of the EC, the EFTA countries acquired a preferred position and consequently a competitive edge over CMEA suppliers.

32

To isolate the effect of the EFTA preferential access to the EC markets we standardised the trade performance for market growth and for changes in relative competitiveness. Changes in competitiveness were isolated by observing the behaviour of both EFTA and CMEA exports to the rest of the world (Young, 1972). The data below (Table 2.3) indicate that despite the lack of preferences, CMEA exporters have actually recorded a better trade performance than was expected on the basis of their relative competitiveness vis-a-vis EFTA-exporters and on the basis of the demand growth in the EC. This is shown by the less than one value of the ratio (15.8/18.2) : (14.5/12.8).

Table 2.2 :   Trade effects of the first enlargement of the EC as a percentage of the 1970 actual exports to the enlarged Community.
(semi-manufactures and finished manufactures only).

CMEA	-15.9
USA	-21.8
UK	+27.3
Continental EFTA	+26.7
Other Developed Countries	
Commonwealth	-22.4
Rest	-20.3
LDCs	-13.1

Source: M.E.Kreinin, The static effects of EEC enlargement on trade flows *Southern Economic Journal*, April 1973, table 3.

Table 2.3 :   Relative export performance of EFTA and CMEA in the EC 1973-1982   (annual rates of change).

Exporting Area	EEC	Rest of World
EFTA	15.8	14.5
CMEA	18.2	12.8

Source: Eurostat Monthly External Trade Bulletin and Secretariat of the European Free Trade Association, EFTA trade, various years.

Thus, it appears that the first enlargement of the EC in 1973 and the simultaneous formation of a free trade area in industrial products between the (remaining) Continental EFTA countries and the EC-9 produced a stronger net trade diverting effect against CMEA exports of manufactures than the formation of the EC-6.

Since differential trade barriers are particularly evident in trade in textiles and clothing we have further compared the export performance of one major group of suppliers of such products with substantial preferential treatment in the EC markets, namely the Southern European countries to the export record in the EC of the CMEA countries over the period 1973-82. Here, one finds considerable evidence that the CMEA countries have actually been hurt by the preferential treatment the Community grants to Southern European exporters of both clothing and textiles (the values of the two overall ratios exceed 10 in both cases). These products, however, account for a small part (around 7%) of CMEA exports to the EC.

Table 2.4: Relative Export Performance of Southern Europe and CMEA in the EC : 1973-1982 (annual rates of change).

	Importing Area	
Exporting Areas	EC	Rest of World*
A. TEXTILES		
Southern Europe	23.5	2.6
Eastern Trading Area	16.5	18.1
B. CLOTHING		
Southern Europe	22.5	9.3
Eastern Trading Area	21.0	88.9

* Rest of World includes : EFTA, USA, Canada and Japan

Source: GATT, International Trade, 1982/83.

The evidence provided so far is certainly not comprehensive but it does permit us tentatively to conclude that apart from agricultural trade, textiles and clothing, the proliferation of EC preferences to third countries does not constitute a serious obstacle to continued expansion of CMEA exports.

A further indication of the ability of the Eastern European exporters to overcome the trade discriminating effects of Western customs unions and preferential trade agreements is provided by comparing the performance of Eastern European exports to the EC with exports of similar products from countries enjoying preferential access (associated or similar status) in the Community markets. Observing the development of market shares in EC imports of raw tobacco between 1960-70, Kebschull (1976) had noticed that despite their association agreements with the Community, Greece and Turkey had not succeeded in increasing their share whereas Bulgaria had managed for most of this period to expand its share substantially above its 1960 level. Brada and Wipf (1976) found that throughout the 1960s the market share of Romania (a non-associated country) has improved vis-a-vis Greek and Turkish market shares in France, Germany and Italy. In both these cases the tariff preferences were not enough to enable Greek and Turkish exports to improve their position relative to either Bulgarian exports of raw tobacco or Romanian total exports.

4 The impact of the second enlargement of the EC on Eastern bloc trade : the case of Greece

As it has already been pointed out in the previous section, any extension of a customs union is bound to change the relative competitive position of the exports of third countries vis-a-vis first, the exports of new members in the markets of the established customs union and secondly, the exports of the members of an established customs union in the markets of the new members. The reason is that following the enlargement exporters from the member countries of the enlarged customs union will now trade with one another on a duty free basis whilst exporters from third countries will still have to face the tariff and other non-tariff barriers of the common external commercial policy of the customs union (Tinbergen, 1960). In this section we examine the extent to which (a) Eastern bloc exports to Greece have suffered from these relative discriminatory effects following the accession of Greece to the European Community and (b) Greek exports have been diverted from Eastern bloc countries to the now more attractive markets of the EC-9.

The evolution of trade shares during the post-accession period is shown in tables 2.5 and 2.6. The data are derived from Eurostat sources and cover the period 1980 (the last pre-accession year) to 1983 (January-June). The data indicate that during this period a substantial reorientation has taken place in the geographical structure of Greek foreign trade.

Looking first at the import side, we notice that the major reorientation of trade flows has taken in the trade in agricultural products. The European Community accounted in 1980 for about 40% of all

35

Greece's imports of agricultural products. In 1981 this share has risen to 72% and during 1983-I to 78%. At the same time whilst in 1980 the share of Eastern Europe in Greece's imports of agricultural products was 22%, it dropped to 3% in 1981 and 2% in 1983-I. The information contained in tables 2.5 and 2.6 does not enable us, strictly speaking, to attribute the reorientation of trade flows entirely to the relative discrimination produced by the extension of the EC customs union to include Greece. To be able to do so we need additional information regarding any changes in the competitive position of the Eastern bloc countries vis-a-vis the EC suppliers. However, as far as agricultural trade flows are concerned it is apparent that this dramatic reorientation of trade flows cannot be explained by changes in the supply capability of the relative competitive position of the Eastern bloc countries. This is a clear case of trade diverted under the influence of the highly protective trade instruments practised within the Community's Common Agricultural Policy.

Table 2.5: Changes in the Shares of the EC and Eastern Europe in Greek Imports: 1980-1983-I (percentages).

SITC	EC	Eastern Europe
0,1	+95	-91
5,6,7,8	+16	-43
Total (excluding oil)	+25	-50

Source : Eurostat

Table 2.6: Changes in the Shares of the European Community and Eastern Europe in Greek Exports : 1980-1983-I (percentages)

SITC	EC	Eastern Europe
0,1	+2	-46
5,6,7,8	+33	-42
Total	+18	-43

Source : Eurostat

The diversion of trade from Eastern bloc countries (inclusive of Yugoslavia) was principally concentrated in the trade in beef. Greek imports of beef from Eastern Europe declined from 33 million kgs in

36

1980 to 2 million kgs in 1981 and 1982. Beef imports from the EC increased from 19 million kgs in 1980 to 55 million kgs in 1981 and 103 million kgs in 1982.

Regarding trade in manufactures, the evidence is more difficult to interpret. One is tempted again to argue that part of the reduction of the share of the Eastern bloc countries in Greek imports during the post-accession period represents trade diverted from CMEA countries to EC suppliers.

Equally difficult is the interpretation of the data on the changing shares of Eastern bloc countries in Greece's exports. Is this reduction in market shares due to the diminishing import absorption capacity of the Eastern bloc countries or is it due to export diversion to the relatively more remunerative markets of the Community? Whatever the explanation, the evolution of trade flows in the post-accession period confirms earlier findings by Thorbecke and Pagoulatos (1975) that the trade diversion of the CAP affects particularly heavily the CMEA countries and indicates that accession to the EC has weakened the trade links of Greece with the CMEA area.

The CMEA share in Greece's external trade was already before accession on a declining trend. It is probable that this declining trend may also be related to the impact of the EC-Greece association treaty and the progressive liberalisation of Community-Greek trade that it entailed.

5 Concluding Remarks

The formation of the European Community customs union produced modest net trade diverting effects against CMEA exports to the EC. Only two other groups of countries (the Continental EFTA countries and the group of other developed countries excluding the USA and the UK) had a similar impact on their trade with EC-6. The negative effect from the formation of the Common Market was, according to Balassa's estimates, approximately equivalent to 4% of the value (at 1959 prices) of the European Community's imports from the CMEA in 1970. This is about half of the relative size of the net trade diverting effect experienced by the group of the 'other developed countries'. The first enlargement of the EC produced stronger net trade diverting effects in the sphere of industrial products - around 16 per cent of the value of the CMEA manufacturing exports to the enlarged EC in 1970 compared to around 10 per cent only during the formation of the customs union among the original six. Again, the (negative) Common Market effect against CMEA exports appears to be less pronounced than the similar negative effect on trade flows originating from either

37

the USA or the group of 'other developed countries'. This is not surprising given the fact that the trade of CMEA countries is governed by intergovernmental agreements.

The relative impact of the Common Market on EC imports from CMEA differs from one product group to another. Net trade diverting effects were particularly serious (in relative terms) in food and beverages, in chemicals and in the SITC groups 6 and 8 (other manufactures). Other product groups, irrespective of whether they had originated from CMEA or elsewhere, had consistently experienced external trade creation effects. Thus, depending on the composition of their exports to the EC some CMEA countries have actually benefited on balance from the trade expansion effects produced by the European Community. The picture one gets from the analysis of the trade data during the formative years of the EC does not appear to hold for the recent southwards enlargement of the Community as shown by Greece's experience in the EC so far.

The proliferation of the EC's preferential trade agreements with various groups of countries place CMEA exporters at increasingly disadvantageous market access conditions. However, apart from the special case of food products, textiles and clothing the multiple trade discrimination system followed by the Community does not seem to have exerted a restrictive influence on EC-CMEA trade. CMEA exporters appear to have managed to overcome the damaging effects of the commercial policies of the EC by linking issues, bargaining for loopholes and mobilising transnational and transgovernmental allies, i.e. through actions similar to those described by Yoffie (1981) as utilised by a number of NICs in overcoming the effects of new protectionism. It could be argued that state trading can be used more effectively as an instrument of linkage politics. One instance of linking issues is the growth of industrial cooperation agreements. It has been estimated (Bulletin, 1980) that about twenty per cent of the growth of East-West trade by 1980 has come from industrial cooperation agreements. Such agreements are particularly extensive in chemicals. Indeed, the growth of a number of restrictions on EC-CMEA trade in chemicals seems to have affected little Eastern exports of chemicals to the West.

One cannot discuss East-West trade in Europe by focusing exclusively on the formation of the European Community customs union. The strong effects of the CMEA customs union on intra-CMEA trade have also produced an adverse impact on EC-CMEA trade. Hewett (1976) has demonstrated that the level of intra-CMEA trade is above typical western intra-trade in both the EC and EFTA. These strong trade creation effects of the CMEA have adversely affected the growth of

East-West trade in Europe far more than the discriminatory effects against third countries generated through the formation of the EC customs union and the Community's preferential trade agreements with EFTA and several other countries. It can also be argued that the negative Common Market effect against CMEA exports could have been mitigated had the economic system of the centrally planned economies of the USSR and Eastern Europe possessed enough flexibility to adjust production towards products benefiting from the external trade creation effects generated particularly during the period of the formation of the customs union of the original six members.

CHAPTER THREE

The Second Enlargement of the EC and the Trade Interests of the Developing Countries.

1 Introduction

The second enlargement of the EC to include three Southern European countries (Greece, Spain and Portugal) will affect the trade interests of the developing countries (LDCs) in two distinct ways. On the positive side, enlargement will extend the geographical frontiers of the preference area within which LDCs' exports are granted favourable treatment. None of the new member-states offered in the pre-accession period preferential market access to LDCs' exports as they neither operated Generalised Systems of Preferences (GSP) except that Greece and Spain were parties to the Protocol of Trade Negotiations Among Developing Countries. By joining the Community, they acceded to the association and trade preference agreements of the EC with various groups of LDCs as part of the *acquis Communautaire*.

There will, however, be another effect of the second enlargement of the EC which will have adverse repercussions on the trade interests of LDCs. The new enlargement of the EC reduces the value of the preferences that several exports from a number of LDCs enjoy in Community markets. Although the conditions of access to the markets of the Community differed before accession between the three newcomers and different groups of products, for a variety of goods several LDCs enjoyed a similar, or in several cases a more favourable, treatment for their exports compared with either all or at least one of the new member states. Given this pre-accession state of affairs with regard to market access to the Community, it becomes important to establish the circumstances under which a group of countries (i.e. the LDCs), which already formed part of a trade preference area with the EC-9, can be damaged by an extension of the customs union to include other countries (i.e. the three new member-states with a pattern of trade similar to that of the preference receiving countries). The damage from the extension of the customs union from the old nine members to the present twelve is referred to in this chapter as the preference erosion or preference dilution effect of the enlargement (for a formal definition see introduction to this volume).

In this chapter an attempt is made to indicate the likely size of these two opposing effects of the second enlargement of the Community on the trade prospects of the LDCs. The first section looks at the relative size of the favourable effect from the extension of the geographical

40

frontiers of the preference area. The subsequent sections single out the major product groups where the erosion of the value of the preferences granted to the LDCs is likely to be serious.

2 The beneficial effects from the extension of the preference area.

Community membership of the three Southern European countries means in almost all cases a unilateral reduction of these countries' tariff levels on imports from third countries. With a few exceptions, the average tariff rates on imports of manufactures into the three new Community countries were before accession to the EC higher than the corresponding Common External Tariff (CET) levels (Commission of the European Community, 1976, 1978a, 1978b). The gradual downwards adjustment of the tariff rates of the three countries towards the CET level will give rise to trade expansion effects. This advantage from the lowering of the tariffs of the three countries on imports from third, non-member, countries will however be shared by the Developed Market Economies (DMEs) and the LDCs alike. The advantage which will be specific to the LDCs is the acccession of the three countries to the complex network of the association and trade preference agreements that the EC maintains with several groups of LDCs. Before we examine the significance of this extension of the geographical boundaries of the EC preference area, it is advisable to urge some caution on the likely expansion of trade from the downwards adjustment of the pre-accession tariff rates of the three countries to the level of the Community's CET.

A careful examination of the tariff structures of the three new members shows that the most important divergencies between their pre-accession levels and the corresponding CET level tend to be found precisely in those products which already compete successfully with LDCs' exports in Community or third markets. High tariff rates considerably in excess of the corresponding CET rates are found in commodity groups where the three countries have high indices of 'revealed' comparative advantage (Yannopoulos, 1980). This state of affairs seems to suggest that tariff rates are used in some instances by the governments in the three new member states not so much as instruments of infant industry protection and of import substitution policies, but as means to enable important groups of local producers to practise market segmentation and geographical price discrimination (Tovias, 1979a). If this explanation of the tariff policies of the three new member countries is correct, then it implies that realignment of the local tariff structure to the CET will not produce significant trade expansion effects. Such a downwards adjustment will simply reduce the profit margins of the protected manufacturers to normal levels.

41

Furthermore, assuming that unutilised capacity exists in the protected industries, the increase in the quantity demanded that will result from the fall in the price paid by the local consumers will be to a large extent met by local production rather than through imports. Thus the trade expansion effects from the downwards adjustment of the tariff levels of the three to the CET level will not be as large as suggested by the pre-accession tariff differentials.

The application of the special terms of the association and trade preference agreements of the Community to the trade of the three new member-countries with the LDCs will affect not only the size of their imports of manufactures but also their trade in agricultural products. If we concentrate for the moment on manufactures, it is obvious that the extent to which the LDCs can penetrate the markets of the new EC members depends above all on the ceilings at which the relevant duty-free quotas are set.

It must be pointed out that the LDCs' exporters of manufactures with duty-free access to the markets of the three new EC members will not be the only ones with preferential access to these markets. As it happens, the three countries have also acceded to the EC agreement establishing a free trade area with the EFTA members that did not join the Community at the time of its first enlargement. Thus LDCs' exporters of manufactures will find themselves competing in the markets of the Three on equal terms not only with producers from the EC-9 but also with producers from EFTA countries. In other words, LDCs' exports of manufactures will be preferred in the markets of the Three only in relation to exports from non-European DMEs. Because of the free trade agreement of the Community with the members of EFTA that stayed outside the EC in 1973, LDCs' exports will enjoy an advantage only vis-a-vis 22.5 per cent of the total manufacturing imports of Greece and Spain (Portugal is excluded from this comparison since it had been a member of the free trade area formed between the EC and EFTA). (Table 3.1). The intra-European free trade arrangements imply a dilution of the preferential status of the LDCs by about 28 per cent - that is, equal to the proportion of the EFTA imports in the combined share of the non-European DMEs and EFTA in the manufacturing imports of Greece and Spain.

A rough method that can be used to provide an indication of the extent to which LDCs can penetrate the markets of manufactures in the three new member states by exploiting the preferential status they will acquire, is to compare the share of the LDCs in the manufacturing imports of the Three with the corresponding share in the imports of manufactures of the Nine. Perhaps a more relevant comparison is with the share of LDCs' manufactures in the imports of Italy. Italy

42

presents considerable similarities with the Three both from the point of view of the cost structure and from the point of the pattern of demand and production. The Italian experience gives us a good benchmark to judge how far one could expect increasing penetration by LDCs' exports into the markets of the Three after these countries grant a preferential status to these exports similar to that granted by Italy.

Table 3.1 : Geographical Origin of Imports of Manufactures in the Three New Member States

	The Three	Greece and Spain
	percentages	
EFTA	50.1	60.1
EFTA	9.3	8.7
The three new member countries	2.4	1.4
Non-European DMEs	20.8	22.5
LDCs	3.7	4.1
Total (in million of US $)	15,412	12,595

Source: OECD, Statistics of Foreign Trade, Trade by Commodities, market summaries: imports, Jan-Dec. 1977, Paris 1979.

Table 3.2 below shows the shares of LDCs' manufactures in the total manufacturing imports of the Nine as a group, of Italy and of the Three new member countries. The share of Ireland is also shown. Ireland is closer to the acceding countries in terms of per capita income but her recent membership status and her different pattern of demand do not make her a good benchmark in predicting the likely change in the share of the LDCs' manufactures in the manufacturing imports of the Three.

The LDCs have shares in the manufacturing imports of all the new member countries which are considerably below those of either the EC-9 or of Italy. If the reasoning given above for the choice of the Italian share as a proper benchmark to judge future developments is accepted, then it may not be unrealistic to expect that by the middle of the next decade (when all transitional arrangements will be completed) the share of the LDCs in the imports of manufactures of the three new member states will reach twice its present level. If indeed the LDCs' share in the imports of manufactures of the three new member countries reaches a level somewhere between the EC-9 average and the

43

Italian one then, at the 1977 level of the manufacturing imports of the three new members it will have amounted to between US $493 million and US $586 million of additional trade. In other words, if the three new member countries were already members of the Community in 1977 and had adopted the EC preferential trade agreements with the LDCs for as long as the present Community members, then the exports of the LDCs would have expanded by around US $500 million at 1977 prices. To keep this change into perspective, it is worth noting that this increase would still have represented about 0.2 per cent of the combined imports of manufactures of the EC-9 and the Three.

Table 3.2: Share of LDCs' Manufactures in Total Manufacturing Imports, 1977

	%
EC-9	6.9
Italy	7.5
Ireland	2.8
Greece	3.3
Portugal	3.7
Spain	4.5
The three new member states	3.7

Source: OECD, Statistics of Foreign Trade, Trade by Commodities, Market summaries: imports, Jan-Dec. 1977, Paris 1979.

3 The erosion of the value of preferences granted to LDCs

The second enlargement of the European Community will disturb the complicated hierarchy of trade preferences that the Community has established over the years with its trading partners in the Mediterranean region and the developing world. The elimination of tariffs and other non-tariff barriers between the Community and the three new member countries will erode the preferential treatment of imports from other developing countries particularly from those which enjoyed a similar or even a more advantageous place in the preference hierarchy of the EC system of external economic relations. The existing system of trade preferences has shaped a certain pattern of price competition between the exports of the three new member

44

countries and similar exports from the LDCs. The erosion of the value of preferences granted to the exports of the LDCs is likely to change their relative competitive position vis-a-vis similar products from the new member countries.

It must be pointed out, however, that for many product groups, exports from the new member countries already have better terms of entry into the Community markets than similar products from LDCs with either association or trade preference agreements with the EC. Manufactures from Greece and Portugal have enjoyed duty-free entry to the Community markets for a number of years before EC membership. It may then be maintained that LDCs have already suffered a dilution of the value of their preferences and that the danger of any further dilution is unreal. There are however several reasons why there is going to be a real erosion of the value of preferences to LDCs from the second enlargement of the Community. In the case of Greece, the products of the iron and steel industries were not covered by the 1961 association agreement. For both Greece and Portugal, exports of textiles to the Community were subject to voluntary export restraints and quota arrangements. Most important of all, the 1970 EC-Spain agreement did not offer to Spanish exports of manufactures duty-free access but only reduced CET rates; some items like cotton yarn and thread, cork manufactures, pile and chenille fabrics and iron and steel products were not covered by the trade preference agreement, whilst others, such as exports of cotton and some petroleum products, enjoyed only a quantitatively limited preferential treatment (Donges, 1976). Furthermore, the preferences granted to Spanish exports (i.e. the percentage reduction of the CET) were often smaller than the corresponding CET reductions on manufactures from the LDCs. Exports of textiles from the Maghreb countries and Malta enjoy free entry while Spain's exports are granted a 60 per cent CET reduction (Tovias, 1979b). Given the importance of Spain as a supplier of manufactures it is not difficult to see that enlargement will give rise to preference erosion effects against some developing countries (see the more detailed analysis in chapter six).

In agricultural trade too, important categories of agricultural exports from the three countries, and in particular from Spain, did not enjoy before accession a better entry status than similar products originating from competing Mediterranean countries. Refined olive oil from the Maghreb countries enters the Community market at a reduced variable levy, whereas similar exports from Spain and Greece were subject to a full variable levy plus a 20 per cent ad valorem duty. Spanish exports of oranges during the October-March period were charged with a 20 per cent ad valorem duty compared to 8 per cent for Israel and 4 per cent for the Maghreb countries (Tovias, 1979b). Agricultural and other primary products (except fuels) constituted nearly one third of the value of all EC imports from the three new member countries before enlargement. A free market in agricultural products between the EC-9 and the Three is bound to dilute the value of the preferences granted to the agricultural exports particularly of the non-acceding Mediterranean countries.

Having established that the potential danger for the LDCs from preference erosion effects is real, let us now examine how far this danger will actually materialise and in which product groups in particular. In this section we look at manufactures. In the following section (and more extensively in the next chapter), the special case of the trade in agricultural goods will be discussed.

At a first approximation it can be maintained that the extent to which suppliers of manufactures from the three new member countries will displace less preferred LDCs' suppliers in Community markets will depend on the margin of preference these suppliers actually acquired upon accession, on the export supply elasticities in the new member countries and on the elasticities of substitution between their exports and LDCs' exports. All three new-member countries are semi-industrialised, middle income, developing countries. Their manufacturing exports are likely to overlap considerably with the type of manufactures that preference receiving LDCs export. But the erosion of the value of the preferences granted to the LDCs will not depend entirely on the extent to which the new member countries are the main competitors of the beneficiary LDCs in the markets of the EC and/or in the markets of the EFTA countries that form part of the free trade area between these two groups of European nations. An equally important factor that will determine the degree of erosion of the trade preferences is the extent to which there exist non-preferred countries exporting into the Community markets at Most Favoured Nation (MFN) rates of tariff products similar to those supplied by the LDCs. After all, as Kreinin (1974) pointed out, preferential treatment is of value if there are major suppliers against whom the beneficiary countries are preferred. There are two groups of countries that export to the Community at MFN tariff rates: the non-European DMEs (USA, Japan, Canada, Australia, South Africa and New Zealand) and the centrally planned economies of Eastern Europe (with the exception of Romania which is accorded GSP treatment). Since price competition is not an important factor in determining the volume of exports of the Eastern European countries, it follows that the main issue here is the degree of overlap between the exports of the preference receiving countries and of the non-European DMEs. Now, if the manufactures exported by the new member countries to the EC are close substitutes with those exported by the preference receiving

LDCs, and if at the same time these exports from the LDCs are also close substitutes of the manufactures exported to the Community by the non-European DMEs, then the competitive advantage gained by the new member countries will affect adversely the market share of the non-European DMEs leaving the value of the preferences undiluted; in such a case the trade diversion effects of the customs union enlargement will be suffered principally by the non-European DMEs.

Factor endowment differences between LDCs and DMEs indicate that the degree of overlapping between the exports of these two groups of countries is likely to be small whilst the overlapping between the exports of the three new members and the LDCs will probably be considerable. Thus it seems that the erosion of the margin of preferences could be substantial although the quantity of trade displaced would not be large given the fact that the three new member countries are not major world suppliers of manufactures.

In order to establish the extent to which the second enlargement of the EC will produce serious preference effects for the manufacturing exports of the LDCs we must look not only at the degree of overlap between the exports of the new member countries and the LDCs but also, at the same time, at the degree of overlap between the exports of the beneficiary LDCs and the non-European DMEs. From this point of view we can classify the imports of the European Community from the three groups of countries so far distinguished (the three new member-states, the LDCs and the non-European DMEs) into eight categories depending on whether the share of these groups of countries in the imports of the EC is small or large (Exhibit 1).

Product groups A to D in exhibit 1 consist of goods in which the share of the non-European DMEs is large in the pre-enlargement period. The trade discrimination effects produced by the extension of the customs union to include the three Southern European countries will most likely be borne by the non-European DMEs and consequently the preferences granted to the LDCs will still be of value after enlargement. Of course, for product groups B and D where the share of the LDCs is already small the preferences do not seem to have been of value to them in any case either because they apply to products that do not fall within the domain of their comparative advantage or because their operation and the restrictive terms under which they are subjected have not allowed the LDCs to penetrate the EC markets significantly. For similar reasons products falling within group E are not likely to suffer serious preference erosion effects, although any trade diversion effect that may still take place will to a certain extent work against the LDCs as well. Products classified into group F are those in which the acceding countries have most likely a strong comparative advantage as revealed by their already large share in the imports of the EC-9. To the extent that they will acquire a competitive advantage after enlargement [1] they are likely to penetrate further the markets of the Community partly at the expense of the LDCs. Because of the strong competitive position of the Three in the products of group F the dilution of the trade preferences is described in the last column of exhibit 1 as serious. But the really serious preference erosion effects will be found in products falling into groups G and H.

Exhibit 1: European Community (EC9) Imports from the Three New Member-States, the LDCs and the Non-European DMEs classified according to their potential preference erosion effects

Product Classification	Share of the Three	Share of LDCs	Share of non-European DMEs	Likely dilution of trade preferences of LDCs
A	S	L	L	insignificant
B	S	S	L	insignificant
C	L	L	L	insignificant
D	L	S	L	insignificant
E	S	S	S	insignificant
F	L	S	S	serious
G	S	L	S	serious
H	L	L	S	serious

S = small import share

L = large import share

The application of the above approach to the actual trade flows can be really useful only in connection with sufficiently disaggregated data. Too high a level of aggregation can give misleading indications. Looking at manufactures as a whole one may be tempted to conclude that the preference erosion effects of the second enlargement of the EC are unlikely to be serious (table 3.3). In 1977, imports from LDCs had a preferential treatment in the markets of the enlarged EC (i.e. EC-9 plus the Three) vis-a-vis 16.8 per cent of all imports of manufactures (= share of non-European DMEs plus of the three new members) on

48

the oversimplified assumption that preferences to LDCs were higher than those accorded to the three new members. After the enlargement the preferential treatment exists only vis-a-vis 14.4 per cent of all imports of manufactures into the EC-12. Such a reduction in the share of non-preferred imports against which LDCs enjoy a tariff advantage can not be regarded as serious. Even more significant appears to be the reduction in the margin of preferences in the markets of EFTA where the LDCs enjoy their GSP schemes whilst the new member countries except Portugal [2] are subject to MFN treatment. Before enlargement, LDCs' exports are preferred vis-avis 12.7 per cent of all manufacturing imports of EFTA; after enlargement the preferential treatment will be vis-a-vis a slightly lower share (11.8 per cent).

Table 3.3: Geographical Origin of Manufacturing Imports EC and EFTA, 1977

	EC-12	EC-9	EFTA
		percentages	
EC-9	62.8	63.0	62.8
EFTA	10.5	10.6	17.0
Three new member countries	2.4	2.4	..
Two new member countries (Greece and Spain)	..	..	0.9
Non-European DMEs	14.4	14.0	11.8
LDCs	6.7	6.9	4.0
Total (in million US $)	237,185	221,773	56,150

Source: OECD, Statistics of Foreign Trade, Trade by Commodities, market
summaries: imports, Jan-Dec. 1977, Paris 1979.

However, a look at more disaggregated data gives a substantially different picture of the preference erosion effects of enlargement. For example, despite the impression of only minor preference erosion effects given from the aggregate data in table 3.3, table 3.4 below shows that for some products like leather the dilution of preferences will be substantial. Accession of the three new members brings the share of non-preferred (or less preferred) leather product imports down from its pre-accession level of 15.9 per cent to only 7.6 per cent, i.e. by more than one half.

Table 3.4 gives the geographical origin of the imports of the EC-9 at the two digit level of the SITC system. Admittedly, this level of disaggregation is also not satisfactory since only at a more refined level of detail it will be possible to detect with a reasonable degree of accuracy the concrete cases where trade erosion effects will actually take place. At the two-digit level of trade classification many dissimilar products with low substitution elasticities may be classed together. But as a preliminary identification of the broad product groups in which preference erosion effects can be expected the analysis at the two-digit level can still give some useful insights.[3] In terms of the classificatory scheme of exhibit 1 the following product categories fall into groups A to E : Paper and paper products (SITC 64), non-metallic mineral manufactures (66), non-ferrous metals (68), non-electrical machinery, electrical machinery and appliances, transport equipment, rubber products (62), iron and steel products (67) and metal manufactures (69). The assignment of these product categories to our groups A to E was made by following a simple rule of thumb according to which a share in the manufacturing imports of the EC exceeding 10 per cent was regarded as a large one and shares below 10 per cent were regarded as small. This obviously introduces some arbitrariness as in the case of the wood and cork products where depending on whether one considers a share of 9.5 per cent as close to the dividing line of 10 per cent, they could be classified as either group D or group F products.

The remaining categories of manufacturing imports i.e. leather products (61), wood and cork products (63), textiles and yarns (65), clothing (84), and footwear (85) fall into groups H and G where the preference erosion effects are likely to be serious. For all these product groups LDCs are substantial suppliers, the three new member countries are also suppliers of some importance and the import shares of the non-European DMEs are rather small and with limits as to the extent they can be brought downwards particularly if account is taken of the product diversities hidden within the two-digit categories. The value of the EC-9 imports from the LDCs in the above five product categories was in 1977 US $6610 million. Since total EC imports of manufactures originating from LDCs were in the same year US $15361 million, it follows that preference erosion will affect 43 per cent of the value of all Community imports of manufactures from LDCs. This is not certainly a development that can be regarded as of minor significance for the trade interests of the LDCs.[4]

In order to obtain an approximate estimate of the quantitative importance of the preference erosion effects we singled out three product categories, textiles, clothing and footwear, and we calculated the potential trade diversion from the enlargement against all third countries. As the preference erosion is expected to be high in these three product categories, it is reasonable to assume that the incidence of the trade diversion will be mainly on the LDCs. The potential trade diversion was estimated (see table 3.5) by assuming that the three new member countries had been able to export the above products to the EC-9 in 1977 at the same relative level as the then 9 member countries.

Table 3.4 : **Geographical Distribution of European Community Imports of Manufactures, 1977**

	Product and SITC category	Total (US $ million)	Percentage		Distribution		
			EC-9	EFTA (excl. Portugal)	Non-European DMEs	LDCs	Non-Member Countries
61	Leather Products	1788	45.0	0.7	9.9	28.2	15.2
62	Rubber Products	2689	77.8	7.1	6.5	2.8	4.4
63	Wood and cork products	2340	43.7	16.0	9.5	19.0	7.5
64	Paper and paper products	7283	45.2	40.4	11.0	0.8	1.2
65	Textiles and yarns	13636	65.2	6.9	5.7	13.4	4.1
66	Non-metallic mineral mfs.	11148	53.7	16.2	12.8	9.3	1.4
67	Iron and Steel	14263	68.8	12.7	8.2	2.6	3.2
68	Non-ferrous metals	11071	44.1	12.1	15.6	22.0	1.6
69	Metal mafs.	7022	70.2	12.2	9.6	3.6	2.6
-	Non-electrical machinery	33543	63.5	12.2	19.6	1.8	1.5
-	Electrical machinery and appliances	20815	59.8	9.9	21.3	5.8	1.7
-	Transport equipment	29877	74.7	5.2	14.3	1.4	3.0
84	Clothing	11166	49.2	4.0	2.3	31.1	6.3
85	Footwear	2656	67.7	5.4	0.7	12.9	8.3

Source: OECD, Statistics of Foreign Trade, Trade by Commodities, market summaries: imports, Jan-Dec. 1977, Paris 1979.

The maximum impact of the preference erosion effect will be when the whole of the potential trade diversion against third countries is borne by the LDCs alone. On the basis of this rather unrealistic assumption, the value of the exports of LDCs lost in the above three product categories would have amounted to US $204 million in 1977. This development from just three product categories would have wiped out about two fifths of the expected trade expansion effects from the extension of the geographical boundaries of the preference area (see section 2 above).

Table 3.5: Potential Trade Diversion against Third Countries : Major Exports of LDCs.

		million of US$	
		Textiles and clothing	Footwear
(A)	Actual EC-9 imports from new member countries, 1977	1269	221
(B)	Hypothetical EC-9 imports from new member countries *	1309	385
(C)	(B) - (A)	40	164
(D)	EC-9 imports from LDCs	5301	343
(E)	(C) as % of (D)	0.8	47.8

*assuming the three new member countries had been able to export the above products in 1977 to the EC-9 at the same relative level as the then member countries (EC-9).

4 The case of trade in agricultural products

Unlike manufacturing imports, where some of the damaging effects from the erosion of the value of preferences will be mitigated by the beneficial effects from the expansion of the preference area, the agricultural exports of the LDCs to the enlarged Community will be subject only to adverse effects. Instead of an extension of the preference area with improved market accessibility which the LDCs will experience in their trade in manufactures they shall face, in the case of agricultural exports, a shrinkage of the world free market area for some of their agricultural products. The main reason for this different impact on the prospects of LDCs' exports of agricultural products is of course the Common Agricultural Policy (CAP). Given the prohibitive variable levy system operated by the Community on

52

grains and livestock products, the markets of the three will become increasingly dominated by suppliers from the EC-9. Thus third country exporters in these temperate zone products will find themselves progressively excluded from the markets of the new member countries. Approximately 73 per cent of imports of meats and live animals, 13 per cent of imports of milk products and 81 per cent of imports of cereals of the three new member countries come from sources outside the EC-9 (Rollo, 1979). However, not many LDCs are producers of temperate zone products but a few, like Argentina, Brazil, Uruguay, that have been exporting to the new member countries will experience the damaging effects of trade diversion. The impact of the prohibitive variable levy system will be reinforced by the inducement effect of the higher support prices that producers in the three new member countries receive in the post-enlargement period. Such higher support prices are likely to stimulate local production, and possibly to cut back the rate of growth of meat consumption (Josling, 1979). The production response from the application of CAP in low income/low price economies could be substantial as the case of Ireland clearly demonstrates (Rollo, 1979). Given the supply situation in the EC-9 and assuming that local production response to higher prices will be short of completely wiping out imports, Community suppliers will be able to displace third country suppliers of pigmeat and dairy products almost entirely and third country suppliers of beef to a considerable extent (Meat and Livestock Commission, 1978).

Table 3.6 :   **Geographical Origin of Selected Agricultural Imports of the EC-9, 1977**

Product and SITC category	Total (US $ million)	Percentage EC-9	EFTA (excl. Portugal)	Non-European DMEs	LDCs	Non-Member Countries
05 Fruit and Vegetables	10470	40.0	0.7	9.9	28.2	15.2
1.12 Wines and Alcoholic beverages	2297	78.5	1.1	1.3	5.1	12.4

Source: OECD, Statistics of Foreign Trade, Trade by Commodities, market summaries: imports, Jan-Dec. 1977, Paris 1979

Preference erosion effects will be noticeable in the fruit and vegetables sector, in wines and olive oil. In these products, entry into the EC will give rise to trade diversion and possibly trade creation in favour particularly of Greece and Spain (Pasca, 1978). LDCs from the Mediterranean region which are the main beneficiaries of preferences in these groups of agricultural commodities will be principally affected. Using the approach followed in the analysis of the preference erosion effects in the trade in manufactures we see (table 3.6) that both fruit and vegetables and wines fall into those groups (H and G respectively) of exhibit 1 which point out to the development of serious preference erosion effects.

How much then of the trade in agricultural commodities between the EC and the LDCs will be affected by serious preference erosion? In 1977, the EC-9 imported from the LDCs products of SITC groups (food and live animals) and 11 (beverages) valued at US $15272.8 million. Imports of items 05 and 1.12 that are expected to have the value of their preferences seriously diluted amounted to US $3071 million in the same year. It thus appears that only about 20 per cent of the LDCs' exports of agricultural products (excluding tobacco) to the Community will be faced with preference erosion. This approach, however, underestimates the importance of the preference erosion for two reasons. Firstly, it does not take into account the fact that the import trade of the Community is heavily concentrated in the countries of the Mediterranean basin. Thus the incidence of preference erosion will be on a limited number of countries. For example, 33 per cent of EC imports of fresh tomatoes come from Morocco (1977); about 40 per cent of imports of olive oil are from Tunisia (1977); 32 per cent of imports of new potatoes come from Cyprus (1977). Only in a few products of the fruit and vegetables sector is the share of non-preferred countries in the Community imports large enough to indicate that the incidence of the trade diversion effect will be on the non-European DMEs. But in most cases, the non-preferred suppliers are Southern hemisphere countries (table 3.7). Only in the case of lemons the expected expansion of the market share of the new member countries would be at the expense of a non-preferred DME, namely the USA. Secondly, the erosion of the margin of preferences will differ depending on the price regime applicable to the various products. Products subject to a reference (minimum import) price regime will tend to be more regularly excluded from the markets of EC-9 than products subject to a tariff regime. In the former case, the additional supplies from the new member countries will give rise more often to the conditions of oversupply that bring about the application of countervailing duties. In the cases where the reference price regime applies we may wish to talk about market exclusion rather than preference erosion. However, as Rollo (1979) points out, the uncertainties about how exactly reference prices work creates ambiguities about the precise form the losses will take. On the other hand, for the products that are subject to a tariff regime, the preference erosion effects will work as described in the case of manufactures in the previous section. But agricultural products coming under a mere tariff regime are rather few (potatoes, cotton-seed, processed fruit, flowers, lamb, mutton, horsemeat).

It is clear from the above that the diversion of the Community's imports from preference receiving LDCs to the new member countries will, in a number of cases, exert a depressing influence on their prices on world markets leading to a deterioration in the terms of trade of these LDCs.

Table 3.7 : Share of Countries not enjoying Preferences in Extra-EC Imports of Selected Agricultural Products, 1977.

Product	Source	%
Oranges	South Africa	7
Lemons	USA	19
Grapes	South Africa	12
Apples	South Africa	21
	Argentina	17
	Australia	6
Pears	South Africa	39
	Australia	8

Source: Eurostat, Foreign Trade Analytical Tables

5 Concluding Comments

A more accurate estimation of the preference erosion effects of the Community's second enlargment can be obtained by refining the level of disaggregation in two directions. First, a finer disaggregation of the commodities covered will enable us to trace more accurately the cases where the elasticities of substitution between alternative sources of imports are high. Secondly, a further subdivision of the geographical origins of the Community's imports would also be useful. Such a subdivision will mainly involve the splitting of EC imports from LDCs into subgroups differentiated by the level of preferences enjoyed in Community markets. Thus imports originating from LDCs could be subdivided into the following groupings: LDCs without any preferences (e.g. Hong Kong); LDCs with only GSPs; LDCs with special trade agreements (e.g. Yugoslavia); LDCs -

members of the ACP group (Lomé) and LDCs from the Mediterranean basin. This subdivision is helpful in determining in a more precise manner the geographical incidence of the trade diversion effects of the recent enlargement and particularly whether there will a shift of the enlarged Community's sources of supply within the group of LDCs, i.e. from LDCs with a low degree of preferences to LDCs with more extensive trade preferences (e.g. from non-ACP to ACP countries). These suggestions are taken up in the next chapter where trade in agricultural products is examined in more detail.

Notes

(1)   The magnitude of the competitive advantage gained will differ from product to product and from one new member state to another. If the product was already entering the EC-9 on a duty-free basis no further competitive advantage will be gained unless accession will eliminate any non-tariff barriers that may have been applying against that particular product. A further question - not explored in this chapter - is the extent to which the three acceding countries will gain a competitive advantage in the markets of some LDCs which have granted reverse preference to the Community (see however chapter 5). This may affect Israel particularly adversely, given the differences between money wage rates in Israel and in the three new member countries (Gutmann, 1984).

(2)   Some of the EFTA countries have granted GSPs for a number of years to Greek manufacturing exports.

(3)   For a more disaggregated analysis see subsequent chapters in this volume.

(4)   A 1981 study by SELA (a coordinating body set up by the Latin American States) gives similar results to our own for Latin American countries separately. According to the SELA report, 33 per cent of EC-9 imports from Latin American countries are vulnerable to preference erosion. The same study gives estimates of the proportion of vulnerable Latin American exports to the three new member states of the EC expressed as a proportion of the total imports of these three countries from the Latin American region. The shares of vulnerable imports are 51% in the case of Spain; 53% in the case of Greece and 70% in the case of Portugal. The higher proportion of vulnerable imports by the Three from Latin America is related to the fact that they are in their majority CAP products whose trade barriers will rise sharply as the trade regime of the CAP is adopted by the newcomers (Ashoff, 1982).

CHAPTER FOUR

The Impact of the Common Agricultural Policy (CAP) on Developing Countries following the Enlargement of the European Community

1 Introduction

One aspect of the second enlargement of the European Community is the extension of the rules of the Common Agricultural Policy (CAP) to the three Southern European countries. The application of the principles of the CAP with its common market organisation and Community preference is bound to have effects not only on the agricultural trade between the three new members and the Community of the Nine but also on the agricultural trade between the enlarged Community and the rest of the world. At the time that the world community is striving (following the developments of the Tokyo round of multilateral trade negotiations and the forthcoming GATT round of MTN) to liberalise world agricultural trade, the second enlargement of the EC will further shrink the share of agricultural production and trade that is exposed to international competition and open to free trade. In this chapter an attempt is made to assess the impact from the extension of the CAP to the three Southern countries on the trade in agricultural products between the enlarged Community and the developing countries. The focus of the chapter is on the impact from the application of the CAP to Southern European agriculture on the prospects for the agricultural exports of the developing countries (LDCs). The analysis here disregards any transitional arrangements that have been agreed with the new members. This exercise shows in other words the situation that is likely to develop when the agricultural sector of all three countries becomes completely integrated into the Community.

The chapter is organised in three main parts. In the first, introductory part, we discuss the major interrelationships that have developed between the CAP and Third World countries. The short second part looks at the basic characteristics of the agricultural structures and the agricultural trade of the three new members. The third part, the more substantive one, indicates the agricultural trade conflicts that are likely to arise as a result of the second enlargement of the European Community.

57

2 The Common Agricultural Policy and the Developing Countries : Some General Considerations.

It has been widely accepted that the CAP is not fundamentally compatible with the interests of the Third World (El-Agraa, 1980a, p. 154). Its extensive use of trade control instruments as a means of supporting and stabilising domestic markets, its excessively high level of overall protection (Sampson and Yeats, 1977) and its wide use of variable import levies and export subsidies have substantially restricted access to the Community markets by Third World (and other) agricultural exporters, depressed the level of world prices in a number of products of export interest to developing countries and accentuated the instability of world markets in a number of agricultural products. Neither restricted market access nor depressed world price levels in agricultural products and increased market instability are in the interests of developing countries - particularly those that are or could potentially become exporters of agricultural products.

As the nature of market organisation and the method of ensuring Community preference varies within the CAP from one product to another (Fennell, 1980), the impact of the CAP is felt differently by different countries. It is basically the producers of temperate zone and Mediterranean type of produce in the Third World that are particularly affected. LDC producers of non-temperate zone products with very close temperate zone substitutes (e.g. sugar, vegetable oils) are also affected. Other tropical product growers are not directly affected by the operation of the CAP although the tariff escalation built into the CET structure creates obstacles to the local processing of such products. As the main support of the CAP is concentrated on cereals and livestock products it is expected that the major impact of the CAP on world markets will be felt by countries exporting such products. Not many LDCs are major cereals and livestock products exporters although it is worth noting that for a number among the poorest of them such products do constitute a sizeable proportion of their total exports. Beef products account, for example, for 41 per cent of Botswana's exports (average 1973-75), for 21 per cent of Upper Volta's and for around 14 per cent of Somalia's, Chad's and Niger's exports. Wheat and beef products accounted for about 27 per cent of Lesotho's exports (average 1970-74) whilst rice represented approximately 10 per cent of Guyana's export earnings over the period 1972-76. (Harris et al, 1978). Nevertheless, given the structure of the non-exclusively-tropical agricultural exports of the developing countries it is mainly exporters of sugar, vegetable oils, fresh fruit and vegetables, wine, fish and preserved fruit and vegetables that are facing serious problems from the import regimes that the Community operates within the CAP system. Already in 1970 products covered by common market organisations accounted for about one-third of the agricultural exports from developing countries. The implications of the restrictive import regimes of the CAP extend far beyond the reduction in LDCs' potential export earnings. Restricted market access, the inherent uncertainty of the import levy system and the obligation to comply with a reference price subject to periodic reviews discourage long term agricultural planning in LDCs. An environment which is not conducive to investment planning is particularly harmful to those LDCs with a considerable potential for agricultural growth.

Inability to increase foreign exchange earnings through agricultural export expansion often forces upon many LDCs a choice of inappropriate development strategies based on suboptimal import substitution policies - with all the well known implications of such policies (Beissner and Hemmer, 1981).

It would be a mistake to confine the impact of the CAP to the group of developing countries exporters of CAP products. The impact of the CAP on world markets for agricultural produce has a more pervasive effect on the development prospects of all LDCs. The (world) price-depressing and market destabilising effects of the CAP exert an indirect impact on both food exporting and food importing LDCs in that they discourage investment in agriculture. By discouraging investment spending in agriculture where incremental spending by rural communities is high, governments in LDCs are deprived of a powerful weapon to stimulate the non-agricultural sector as well. Thus the solution to the problems of rural unemployment is hindered whilst at the same time negative distribution effects are produced within the LDCs. These adverse effects on agricultural development are further accentuated through the market disturbances caused by food aid policies in recipient countries in view of the link between food aid and CAP-induced surplus disposal.

This is not of course to deny certain benefits that a number of developing countries, particularly food importing ones, can reap temporarily from the operation of the CAP. The expansion of the livestock sector in the EC through the stimulus of high CAP prices generates import demand for animal feed such as cassava and soya bean in view of the relatively more expensive prices for domestically produced cereals (also as a result of the CAP). This interrelationship that exists between livestock products, grains and oilseeds often provides a boost to the development of exports by LDCs that are in a position to supply the markets generated by the CAP supportive system. But is this the best way of improving the impact of the CAP on LDCs? Interdependence between EC agriculture and the agriculture of developing countries could also be encouraged through a CAP relative price structure that increases Community production of cereals, reduces EC production of beef and stimulates LDC sales of grass-fed beef exports. Is this alternative pattern of interdependence economically superior to the current one? Unless we are able to answer such questions it would not be possible to regard as a clear-cut benefit the present pattern of EC - LDC interrelationships in the livestock-grains-oilseeds markets.

It is pointed out that by depressing international grain prices the CAP has generally produced a favourable effect on the terms of trade of cereals importing LDCs. But the variability of international grain prices to which the same CAP policies contribute, tend also to periodically destabilise the terms of trade and thus produce strains on the domestic economies of the cereals importing LDCs (Josling, 1980a). These benefits can hardly compensate for the adverse effects. By severely curtailing the incentives to produce in LDCs, the CAP and similar protective devices of other industrialised countries encourage production in places where the social resource cost of agricultural output is higher and thus reduce the world's global income (Josling, 1979).

3 A Brief Review of the Agricultural Structures of the New Members.

Given that the CAP regime has several crucial implications for the development of agricultural production and trade in LDCs, it is of considerable importance to enquire on the effects from the extension of the CAP mechanism to the agriculture of the three new members on the agricultural exports of the LDCs.

The enlargement of the Community with the addition of Greece, Portugal and Spain has considerably expanded the agricultural sector of the Community. Integration of the agricultural sectors of the three new members with the agricultural sectors of the nine other Community members has increased the agricultural population of the EC by about 55 per cent, the total agricultural land by about 50 per cent (see table 4.1) and the value of agricultural production by a little less than 25 per cent. Enlargement, in other words, cannot be regarded as a marginal operation with insignificant effects on the way the CAP influences development prospects in LDCs.

As the structure of production in the new members is more heavily weighted towards crop products, the competitive advantage to be gained by the three new members in EC markets will be mainly felt by exporters of crop products to the Community. A further glance at the structure of crop production shows that it is in the area of fruit (particularly citrus fruit), vegetables, wine and olive products where the three new members have acquired advantages from specialisation. Exports of these products (plus tobacco in which Greece specialises substantially) from third (other than EC-12) countries to the Community are likely to experience serious market access problems once the CAP is fully operational in the three new members. Exporters of meat products, feed grains and oilseeds from non-EC countries to the three Southern European countries are also likely to face even more serious market access problems as the adherence to the Community preference principle shifts the three members' sources of supply to EC-9 markets.

It is worth noting that although Spain sends already about 70 per cent of her agricultural exports to the Community (EC-9), the other two countries have directed in the pre-enlargement period approximately only two-fifths of their agricultural exports to the EC-9. However, in absolute terms, the value of the remaining 30 per cent of Spanish agricultural exports is almost equal to the value of the 60 per cent of the combined agricultural exports of Greece and Portugal. Now when the three are full members of the Community one expects a further proportion of their exports to be channelled to the markets of the EC-9 at the expense of third country competitors. Potential exports to the EC are likely to further expand not only because of the price incentives that membership offers to the three new members but also because of the existing room for productivity gains in agricultural production. Spain and Portugal offer the largest potential for expansion here both on account of the structure of their land holdings (substantial proportion of agricultural land in holdings of 20ha and over) and also on the basis of the considerable margin they have for increasing their irrigated area (Pepelasis et al., 1980).

4 The Effects of the Enlargement on LDCs Trade Interests

In order to examine the impact of the enlargement of the Community on LDCs' exports of agricultural products it is convenient to distinguish between exclusively tropical products on the one hand and temperate zone and Mediterranean type of produce on the other. This distinction is based on the differences in the import regimes under which the three groups of products enter into Community markets.

Exclusively tropical products are subject to a customs tariff regime only with preferential treatment (reductions of the CET rates) accorded to ACP countries and to a limited range of products to GSP beneficiaries. Since the main change that enlargement will bring about is the alignment of the tariff structure of the three new members to the

61

CET, the impact on LDC exporters of tropical goods will depend on the difference between the tariff rates (and other trade barriers) currently applicable on imports of the new members from LDCs and the corresponding CET rates. Greek pre-accession tariff rates on imports of tropical products were in the majority of cases higher than CET rates. The same is in many cases true for Portugal and Spain. Spain and Portugal have tariff rates below the CET level on imports of vegetables oils and sugar (Donges et al., 1982). A substantial proportion of their import requirements has been provided by Latin American countries. Given the binding EC import guarantees (sugar) and the preferential treatment to be granted to the ACP countries, the completion of the accession of Portugal and Spain will bring a shift of their supply sources from one group of LDCs (Latin America) to another (ACP). However, concern has already been voiced by the ACP countries for the limitations on the quantity of raw sugar Portugal may import from ACP. The limitation is provided for in the Treaty of Accession and is set at 75,000 tonnes. All in all, one would expect that as far as tropical products are concerned a limited trade expansion in favour of LDCs is likely to take place, whilst the granting of preferences to the ACP states will generate some trade diversion against non-preference receiving LDCs (McQueen and Read, 1986b). Even this limited trade expansion may be severely restricted if the new members decide to invoke the safeguard provisions of the Lomé convention. The chance of this happening is not so unreal. Imports to the three new members from the EC-9 are likely to expand more than their exports to the Community. To improve their balance of payments performance the new members may resort to various safeguard devices to control the flow of imports from non-EC sources.

In temperate zone products all three new members are characterised by supply deficiencies and import a considerable proportion of their domestic consumption requirements from third countries outside the EC-9. Spain, in particular, imported around 3/4 of its domestic consumption of meat and coarse grains (Tovias, 1979, p.13). Given the prohibitive CAP variable levy system on grains and livestock products, the markets of the three new members will become progressively dominated by suppliers from the EC-9. Thus third country exporters of these temperate zone products will find themselves eventually excluded from the markets of the new members. Of course, not many LDCs are exporters of temperate zone products but the few, like Latin American countries and Yugoslavia, that have been exporting to the three countries will experience the damaging effects of trade diversion. What is then the likely size of the purchases of cereals and meat that the change in the import regime will channel from third countries to Community suppliers? A relatively recent

62

estimate by Marsh (1978) puts the size of the trade diversion effect (substitution of cereals and meat from the EC-9 for purchase from third countries) at approximately $1,500 mil. at 1975 prices. This redirection of trade will adversely affect the welfare of both third countries and the new members. Suppliers from the Third World will be more severely affected as the scope for sectoral resource reallocations is more limited than in developed economies. The cost of the trade diversion on the new members will not be negligible either. Estimates range from $310 mil. (Kirschke, 1981) to $450 mil. (Marsh, 1978).

The impact of the prohibitive variable levy system will be reinforced by the inducement to expand production in the new members once the higher support prices of the CAP are introduced. Some estimates of the likely expansion of production (together with projected demand changes) are given in table 4.2. What this table shows is the size of the relative change when projections based on the CAP regime are compared to projections without the enlargement effect. Higher support prices will stimulate local production and cut back the rate of growth of a number of meat consumption items.

Table 4.2 shows that for coarse grains, rice, mutton and lamb the positive production response is greater than the demand response - a development likely to lead to trade erosion (negative trade creation). Thus the stimulus given to domestic production in the three new members coupled with the contraction in demand could eliminate all imports from third countries. On the other hand for milk and meat products demand is expected either to expand at a faster rate than domestic production or to contract at a slower pace than the reduction in domestic production.

The situation with regards to Mediterranean produce shifts the focus of attention from the markets of the three new members to the markets of the EC-9. It is in these markets that producers from the Southern European countries that have become the new Community members compete with producers of fruit and vegetables (both fresh and preserved), wine, olive oil and tobacco from LDCs (table 4.3). The three countries compete in the import markets of the EC-9 within a framework of a complicated system of preferential trade and development cooperation agreements. The precise position of the three new members in the hierarchy of preferences prevailing in the EC-9 markets is difficult to establish. Donges et al. (1982, p. 170) calculated the preference margin enjoyed by a group of 11 LDCs from the Mediterranean basin vis-a-vis each of the new members. The results are reproduced in table 4.4   Before enlargement, Greece already enjoyed a higher preferential status in the EC-9 markets vis-a-vis the Mediterranean countries (with the exception of Algeria and Tunisia) whilst Portugal and Spain occupied a lower place relative to the Mediterranean countries in the preference hierarchy of the EC (again with some exceptions for Portugal's trade with Turkey, Lebanon and Jordan, and Spain's trade with Turkey and Lebanon). Since ACP countries enjoy a more preferred import regime in the EC, it appears that Portugal and Spain had a lower margin of preference also vis-a-vis the ACP states.

Enlargement will thus disturb the present hierarchy of preferences under which the new members and the LDCs have been competing in the agricultural import markets of the EC-9 for Mediterranean type of produce. This will produce a preference erosion effect (reversal of tariff preferences) which will undermine the competitive position of the LDCs which export Mediterranean type of produce. Exporters of olive oil from North Africa and Turkey will inevitably face increased competition in the Community's olive oil market. This is particularly the case for Tunisia which sends 78 per cent of its olive oil exports to the EC. Morocco's share of the EC orange market appears seriously threatened if as predicted by the US Department of Agriculture Spain's exports of oranges to the EC increase by at least 9.4 per cent as a direct consequence of enlargement. A similar threat is posed to Morocco's share of the processed tomatoes market. Countries most likely to be seriously affected from the erosion of preferences are those whose structure of agricultural exports to the EC shows a considerable degree of similarity with the corresponding export structure of the new members and that furthermore have a high proportion of agricultural exports in their total exports to the EC. A first indication of the most vulnerable countries could be gained by using the Kreinin-Finger (1979) index of trade similarity (see notes at the end of next chapter). The results of this exercise are shown on table 4.5. Most of them appear vulnerable to the Spanish export thrust in particular.

The way preference erosion will restrict export opportunities for LDCs can be shown by means of diagram A. To simplify the diagrammatic representation we assume the existence of only three trading groups competing in the EC-9 import markets: the new members, the developing countries supplying Mediterranean type of produce and the rest of the world (McCulloch and Pinera, 1977).

In the diagram overleaf curve DME shows the EC's net demand for imports from the three sources. The CET rate is measured by the distance TA. Both the new members and the LDCs enjoy a preferential tariff rate measured by the distance ab($<$ TA). The supply curve for the rest of the world is assumed to be perfectly elastic (S_R) whilst the supply curve of the new members is shown by line S_N

64

DIAGRAM A

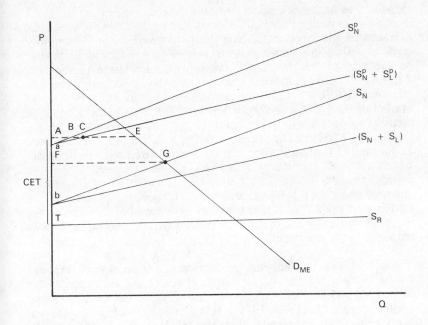

(before the imposition of the preferential duty) and by line S^P_N after the imposition of the preferential duty. The lines $S^P_N + S^P_L$ and $(S_N + S_L)$ represent the combined supply curve of both the LDCs and the new members before and after the imposition of the preferential duty. After enlargement exports from the new members will enter the EC market duty free and consequently the supply response of the producers from the new members is shown by line S_N. Given the cost conditions represented by the supply curves in diagram A and the size of preference erosion the new members will supply all the requirements of the import market of the EC in this product displacing both LDC suppliers and rest of the world suppliers when they fully accede to the Community. Notice that before enlargement the rest of the world was supplying a quantity equal to CE whilst LDC producers were selling a quantity equal to BC. Thus as a result of a change in the structure of preferences considerable changes have taken place in the pattern of EC imports.

However, as becomes evident from the diagram, the extent to which the erosion of preferences will seriously restrict the ability of the LDCs to compete with producers from the new members in Community markets will depend on a number of factors. It will first of all depend on the size of the preference erosion effect relative to the cost differentials between the new members and the LDCs in the products affected. It will, secondly, depend on the extent to which the import market of the EC-9 was supplied, prior to the enlargement, by third country producers with no preferential status, such countries are the Developed Market Ecopnomies (DMEs) and the Centrally Planned Economies of Eastern Europe (CPEs) (with the exception of Romania which is a GSP beneficiary). Whilst enlargement changes the reactive competitiveness of the LDCs vis-a-vis the new members, it also changes to an even larger extent the corresponding position of the DMEs and the CPEs relative to the new members. Finally, the ultimate impact of the preference erosion will depend on the supply response in the new members.

Table 4.2 gives the estimated production and consumption response for two groups of citrus fruit. Similar responses are expected for other fruit and vegetable products particularly tomatoes, onions and winter vegetables (FAO, 1979). It is then reasonable to expect that for a variety of fruit and vegetable products the degree of self-sufficiency of the enlarged EC will increase. This coupled with the fact that the spread of the extra-EC market in most of these products is relatively limited, will lead to downwards pressures on the prices of these goods as the excluded exports of the LDCs will be flooding third markets with limited demand prospects. If export subsidies are made available to the new surplus production, e.g. oranges, then the damage to third countries may prove in some cases more serious than the displacement of these exports from the markets of EC-9. Price variability in the non-shielded world markets for Mediterranean type of produce may also increase. Any downwards pressure on prices in the remaining, non-shielded, world markets will have further repercussions on the income levels of countries whose exports are heavily concentrated in Mediterranean type of products. Braun and Haen (1982) estimated that a ten per cent decline in the prices of fruit and vegetables exported by Egypt will bring about a 2.2 per cent

66

reduction in the value added by her agricultural sector and a 0.4 per cent decline in her national income; whilst a thirty per cent price decline in the export prices of these products will bring about a 6.5 per cent decline in the value added by the agricultural sector and a 1.1 per cent reduction in national income.

The improvement in the position of the three new members in the preference hierarchy of the EC (at least in the case of agricultural trade) will change relative import prices in favour of these countries. Such changes will provide an incentive to the EC importers to switch their sources of supply well away from countries that enjoyed a more favourable position in the EC's preference hierarchy before enlargement to the now more preferred suppliers from the new member countries. If relative import prices change in favour of the new members then, other things being equal, their relative share in the imports of agricultural products of the Mediterranean type by the EC-9 will also rise in their favour. However, it is not certain that any expansion in the market share of the new members in the imports of the EC-9 will be at the expense of the pre-enlargement most preferred sources i.e. the Mediterranean and the ACP countries (Kreinin, 1974). For, although it is true that the import prices of the pre-enlargement most preferred sources of supply will become relatively less attractive vis-a-vis suppliers from the new members nevertheless their relative position vis-a-vis non- or less-preferred sources will not change. Thus, whilst the relative competitiveness of the pre-enlargement most preferred sources of supply will be adversely affected in comparison to the sources of supply from the new members, it will not be influenced in any way in comparison to the sources of supply from non- or less-preferred sources. These changes in the structure of relative prices imply that in those cases where the countries that move downwards in the preference hierarchy of the EC compete in the markets of the EC-9 with no preferred suppliers the value of their preferences is not likely to be eroded since they can still maintain their market share at the expense of the less preferred suppliers. In other words, the trade displacement effects of the second enlargement will be experienced by suppliers from countries without preferences in their agricultural trade with the Community.

In order to isolate such cases from those that will involve a genuine erosion of the trade preferences we examined in detail the geographical origin of the imports of the Community of Nine in 62 product categories corresponding to the six digit NIMEXE code of Eurostat. This detailed commodity classification enables us to deal with homogeneous products as well as to cope with calendar variations in crop production in different parts of the world. To avoid seasonal influences, the average value of imports over the two-year period

1979-80 was taken as the basis for analysis. Imports were then classified into seven regions corresponding more or less to the different levels of preferences that agricultural imports from these sources enjoy in Community markets. The labyrinth-like structure of Community preferences renders any classificatory scheme open to criticisms on a few points but in general it is accepted that suppliers from the ACP and the Mediterranean countries are more preferred than suppliers from either other LDCs or from the developed market economies or the centrally planned countries. Since it is the group of the Mediterranean and the ACP countries that will experience a reduction in their preference status after the second enlargement of the Community is completed we decided to include in our sample products of export interest both to the new members and the ACP and Mediterranean countries. These are essentially Mediterranean type of products. The product categories included in our sample (see table 4.6) represented for the 1979-80 period 19.6 per cent of all EC-9 imports of products in groups 1-24 from the Mediterranean region.

The 62 product categories were then classified into three groups on the basis of the degree of preference erosion that suppliers from the CAP and the Mediterranean countries are expected to experience. Products in **Group A** are of export interest to the new members but either of no interest or of minor interest to the ACP and the Mediterranean countries. Both before and after the second enlargement any preferences to the ACP and the non-candidate Mediterranean countries are practicially of no value to them. A relative reduction in the preferential status of these countries will have no substantial consequence for their extremely limited export interests. However, it is worth noting that a zero or a minute share in the imports of the EC-9 does not necessarily indicate the prohibitive nature of some of the instruments the Community uses in restricting the flow of agricultural trade like the use of calendar restrictions. Products that fall under this group include peaches, cucumbers, pears, treated olive oil, natural honey, preserved asparagus and a few others. From the data in table 4.6 it is clear that any expansion of the exports of the new members in the first two products will be at the expense of (more costly) Community production.

Products in **Group B** include a number of items which are supplied both by the Mediterranean plus the ACP countries and non-preferred sources. In these products the Mediterranean countries in particular appear to be major suppliers to the Community markets but at the same time exporters from non-preferred sources are also major suppliers in the Community markets. The preferences available to the Mediterranean non-candidate countries will thus retain their value after the second enlargement. Several types of fruit and vegetables are included in this category. Again for a number of the products included the limited erosion case holds only for certain periods of the year. Tobacco, currants, grapefruit, the largest part of imported wines, onions and sweet peppers are among the major products included in this group of limited preference erosion.

The substantial erosion group (**Group C**) includes products which are of export interest to the Mediterranean and ACP countries but of no or limited interest to third, non-preferred suppliers. Any export thrust by the new members in these product categories is thus likely to take place at the displacement of the trade of the non-candidate Mediterranean producers. Approximately 45 per cent of the value of imports included in our sample of 62 product categories falls in the group of substantial erosion effects. This represents 9.4 per cent of EC-9 imports in classes 1-24 from the Mediterranean region. The main products included in this list are: tomatoes, several types of citrus fruit, fresh grapes, grape juice, olive oil (untreated), green beans and capers and olives, prepared or preserved.

The ability of third country exporters to sell to the Community markets under the CAP regime is only partially determined by the preference margin that selected groups of suppliers enjoy. The Community's policy on agricultural imports can also be influenced by the manner in which it uses the variety of prohibitive trade instruments it has at its disposal. Reference prices, import licensing and safeguard provisions are likely to operate more forcefully as trade barriers against agricultural imports from third countries in the EC-12. Third country producers will have difficulties in meeting the reference price level as increased supplies from the new members will depress the prices of these products in Community markets. As a situation of oversupply develops in a number of markets, the operation of the import licensing system will become more stringent and safeguards more widely practised. Furthermore, as the Mediterranean regions of France and Italy start experiencing the effects of intensified competition from the new members, such market access limiting devices may be more intensively used in an effort to shift the burden of adjustment to the producers of similar goods outside the Community.

It appears, therefore, that the damaging effects from the erosion of preferences currently enjoyed by the non-candidate Mediterranean countries in particular are not likely to be negligible. Obviously, the extent to which the damaging displacement of trade against these countries will actually materialise depends on the export and production response in the new members. As Gaines, Sawyer and Sprinkle (1981) have shown in their study on the impact of the EC's preferential citrus fruit agreements, the existence of preferences does not necessarily imply that all potential beneficiaries are able to exploit the opportunities open to them. Some production response, particularly in the annual crops, is certain to occur (Josling, 1980b). The need to minimise the damaging effects of trade displacement against the non-candidate Mediterranean and a few ACP countries still remains.

The Community's second enlargement will give rise to new trade conflicts which unlike those generated at the time of the formation of the EC-6 will involve weak and vulnerable economies at a critical stage of their development. A number of options are open to the Community if it decides to rectify the adverse effects of the second enlargement on the agricultural trade particularly of the non-candidate Mediterranean countries. The Community may decide to set up a special export compensation scheme along the lines of the STABEX arrangement to cover a number of the products included in Group C above. Alternatively, the Community may try to promote structural adjustments within its own agriculture so that accessibility to its markets by exporters from the affected countries is eventually improved. Finally, agreed specialisation policies involving both the Community and the countries of the Mediterranean and the ACP may also be explored. The first and third policy options raise a number of difficulties (Duchêne, 1985). The second appears to be more promising. Some rather hesitant steps towards structural adjustment have been taken with the launch of the Integrated Mediterranean Programmes (IMP). One aspect of the IMPs (scheduled for seven years and allocated about 6,600 million ECUs) is to facilitate the implementation of crop-change and conversion schemes and to encourage the development of non-agricultural activities (crafts, tourism) in the rural regions of three Mediterranean member states, i.e. France, Greece and Italy (Commission of the EC, 1983). In the meantime the Community is engaged in a holding operation aiming at the maintenance during the transition period, of the level of the agricultural imports originating in the non-candidate Mediterranean countries at the annual average quantities (termed as traditional quantities) imported during the period 1980-1984. Special arrangements have also been agreed for olive oil from Tunisia. Although the quantities imported during that period have already been affected by Greece's accession, they ensure nevertheless that the Iberian enlargement will not affect adversely the conditions of access to the EC market for the staple exports of Mediterranean countries. What will happen after the transition period is completed remains unclear, except that in the meantime the Commission proposes to phase out the customs duties on the agricultural products of interest to the Mediterranean countries at a speed similar to that agreed for the elimination of duties in respect of Portugal and Spain, up to traditional quantities by country of origin and by product.

Table 4.1: The Relative Importance of Agriculture in the EC-9 and in the Three New Members

	EC-9	New Members		
		Greece	Portugal	Spain
Agricultural Land (1,000 ha) (1976)	93,606	9,140	4,130	31,516
of which : arable land, including permanent crops. (p.c.)	55.3	42.5	87.2	65.5
permanent grassland (p.c.)	44.7	57.5	12.8	34.5
Share of holdings over 20 ha. in total agricultural land (1977). * (p.c.)	72.8	12.1	58.9	80.0
Share of crop production in agricultural output (1977) (p.c.) **	40.2	69.0	65.1	58.9
of which: fruit	(3.8)	(12.3)	(9.7)	(16.7)
vegetables	(7.1)	(4.5)	(12.3)	(9.0)
wine	(4.6)	(2.3)	(10.5)	(3.6)
olive	(1.0)	(7.6)	(5.6)	(2.9)
Share of Livestock production in agricultural output (1977) (p.c.) **	58.9	31.0	34.9	41.1
Share of the EC-9 in total exports of food, beverages and tobacco (1976)	-	43.0	41.0	72.0
Share of Food, Beverages and Tobacco in total exports to EC-9 (1977)	-	27.4	23.7	27.4
Proportion of workforce in Agriculture (1975)	8.2	28.4	32.5	20.7

* for Portugal : 1968 and for Spain : 1972

** for Portugal : 1975 and for Greece : 1976

72

Table 4.2: Enlargement-Induced Production and Demand Shifts in the New Members*

Product	Percentage Change of	
	total production of New members**	total demand of New members
Wheat	+14.3	+14.3
Coarse Grains	+ 9.1	- 11.8
Total Grains	+11.1	- 4.2
Rice	+ 7.0	- 7.0
Milk	+ 4.4	+ 8.0
Beef and Veal	- 2.3	- 1.8
Mutton and Lamb	+ 5.2	- 5.0
Pork	- 11.6	- 6.3
Poultry	- 21.2	+ 2.2
Tobacco	+ 7.3	-
Oranges	+ 3.0	- 5.0
Mandarins, Tangerines and Clementines	+10.0	- 10.6

Source: Food and Agricultural Organisation of the United Nations, Commodity Review
Review and Outlook, 1979/80, FAO Economic and Social Development Series, No. 17, Rome 1979

*   difference between projection to 1990 with and without enlargement

**   base period = annual average 1975-77.

Table 4.3: Geographical Distribution of European
Community Imports of Selected Agricultural
Products, 1978

SITC		TOTAL (US $ million)	PERCENTAGE DISTRIBUTION				
			EEC-9	EFTA excl.Portugal	Non-European LDCs	DMEs	Three New Members
03	Fish & Fish preserved	3162	40.58	14.04	19.83	15.91	4.36
034	Fish,fresh or frozen	1561	49.39	16.78	10.76	17.23	2.31
035	Dried,salted or smoked fish	258	36.82	45.74	2.33	2.71	4.65
036	Crustaceans and molluscs,fresh or frozen or salted	523	36.90	2.10	40.34	9.56	4.02
042	Rice	584	35.27	-	31.51	31.85	1.20
05	Vegetables and Fruit	11723	39.04	0.65	32.41	9.45	15.14
054	Vegetables,fresh and chilled or frozen	3486	48.80	0.75	30.41	3.53	12.85
056	Vegetables prepared or preserved	1276	55.02	0.47	25.00	2.82	12.54
057	Fruit and Nuts, fresh or dried	5252	28.43	0.27	37.24	13.46	18.55
058	Fruit,preserved and fruit prepared	1709	39.91	1.70	26.39	14.10	11.18
112	Alcoholic beverages	3016	79.77	1.39	4.21	1.06	11.41

Source: OECD Trade Statistics

Table 4.4: **Preference Margin of 11 Mediterranean Countries vis-a-vis the New Members in the Agricultural Import Markets of the EEC-9**

	Mediterranean country preference margin vis-a-vis the weighted average EC tariff rate imposed on the same agricultural imports from				Weighted average EC tariff rate imposed on exports of
	Greece	Portugal	Spain	weighted average MFN rate	
Algeria	7.7	12.1	11.7	12.5	6.4
Cyprus	-10.2	3.5	4.1	6.0	12.4
Egypt	- 5.2	1.7	3.7	4.0	10.2
Israel	- 2.2	7.5	4.7	7.5	6.1
Jordan	- 7.0	- 7.0	0	0	7.0
Lebanon	- 2.3	- 0.1	- 0.1	0.2	12.5
Malta	-24.0	2.3	3.9	3.9	35.6
Morocco	- 5.9	5.6	7.9	11.3	5.9
Syria	- 0.1	0.8	0.5	1.0	1.8
Tunisia	4.0	4.6	4.6	5.3	30.3
Turkey	- 1.4	- 0.2	- 0.7	3.6	1.4

Notes:

1. In cases where import variable levies were used, the difference between the intra-EEC import unit value and the extra-EC import unit value for the product was taken as a proxy.

2. Tariff rates have been weighted by the EC import values

3. Average tariff rate imposed under the assumption that the EC-9 imports the same amount of Mediterranean country major agricultural products from the new members.

Source: J.B. Donges, C. Kriger, R.J. Langhammer, K.W. Schatz & C.S. Thoroe, The Second Enlargement of the European Community, JK.C.B. Mohr, Tübingen, 1982.

Table 4.5: Similarity Indexes Between the Structure of
Agricultural Exports to the EC of the Three New
Members and the Mediterranean Region.

Country	Greece	Portugal	Spain
Algeria	59.2	64.9	76.3
Cyprus	57.0	16.4	66.5
Egypt	63.3	0	55.3
Israel	40.2	0	34.4
Jordan	0	0	0
Lebanon	32.2	0	76.7
Malta	40.3	14.4	45.6
Morocco	25.6	11.2	63.0
Syria	32.9	60.3	70.2
Tunisia	63.6	17.1	57.6
Turkey	40.5	6.6	71.4

Note: For details of how this index is constructed see note 2 in chapter 5.

Source : see table 4

Table 4. 6: EC-9 Imports of Selected Agricultural Products by Preference Group (1979-80)

Product Category	Value of Imports (1000EUA)	Shares (in percentages)						
		Intra-EC(9)	New Member	ACP	Mediterranean Countries	Other LDCs	DMEs	CPEs
Group A: No Erosion of Preferences								
Potatoes other than new (NIMEXE 0701.19)	133,408	95.02	6.44	-	1.54	0.05	2.54	0.40
Satsumas and Monreals	66,590	2.26	97.08	-	0.57	0.01	0.06	-
Table grapes (1/11 - 14/7), fresh	99,604	32.12	26.49	-	3.16	3.65	34.58	-
Almonds (sweet	4,530	12.94	21.64	-	3.62	0.34	60.97	-
Apples (1/10 - 31/12)	135,669	89.19	2.57	-	0.21	0.91	6.62	0.47
Apples (1/1 - 31/3)	132,219	88.17	0.47	-	0.08	5.94	4.45	0.79
Apples (1/4 - 31/7)	313,882	47.13	0.06	-	-	21.15	31.55	0.12
Pears (1/4 - 5/7)	47,954	31.75	4.16	-	-	28.71	35.32	-
Peaches	206,388	77.21	20.99	-	0.47	0.64	0.58	0.11
Cucumbers (1/11 - 15/5)	108,680	60.45	36.64	-	0.05	0.10	0.02	2.74
Cucumbers (16/5 - 31/10)	99,658	93.96	3.70	-	0.06	0.01	0.08	2.20
Strawberries (1/5 - 31/7)	112,644	93.93	3.74	-	-	-	0.37	1.93
Treated Olive Oil	13,519	52.79	44.08	2.26	0.25	0.21	-	-
Asparagus preserved	104,490	8.27	4.36	0.05	-	82.76	3.96	0.60
Wines 18-22% vol. exc. porto etc (1)	18,632	87.00	8.83	-	0.57	0.05	3.11	-
Natural Honey	102,241	11.99	3.72	1.36	0.25	43.04	12.60	27.15

Table 4.6 (continued)

GROUP B : Limited Erosion of Preferences

Tomatoes (15/5 - 31/10)	214,384	88.54	3.85	-	5.53	0.01	0.04	2.03
Oranges, fresh sweet: navels, navelines etc. (16/5 - 15/15)	132,024	8.96	6.17	0.81	19.11	10.34	54.53	0.08
Mandarins and Wilkings	8,664	37.84	48.38	1.94	6.89	1.70	3.59	-
Tangerines	4,259	20.62	2.98	0.79	33.11	14.02	24.51	-
Citrus hybrids similar to mandarins etc.(2)	5,350	14.30	7.14	16.43	12.07	16.97	33.03	-
Lemons	137,253	29.25	47.85	0.03	8.80	2.59	11.46	-
Grapefruit	152,811	10.69	0.67	2.79	46.79	8.25	30.33	0.48
Currants	239,494	1,48	35.98	-	29.64	10.10	22.49	0.31
Almonds (bitter)	4,530	5.22	3.66	-	76.20	12.63	2.03	-
Orange juice of a density exceeding 1.33 and more than 30 ECUs per 100 kgs	204,986	18.14	3.47	0.33	22.46	48.41	7.16	-
Wines or fresh grapes not exceeding 15% vol. plus wines flavoured by aromatic extracts of 18% vol or less (3)	1,209,657	82.93	7.23	-	4.14	0.21	2.95	2.53
Wines of fresh grapes strength 15-18% vol. excluding porto etc (4)	23,201	27.56	18.75	-	35.89	0.66	16.24	0.78
Tomatoes, prepared or preserved	212,832	66.60	25.51	-	4.53	0.28	0.74	2.32
Onions	154,576	56.34	26.62	-	5.94	2.98	5.25	2.87
Sweet peppers	101,445	53.23	27.59	2.06	10.99	0.99	1.12	4.96
Strawberries (1/8 - 30/4)	46,492	54.36	17.67	-	13.14	5.60	9.04	0.17
Flowers	673,165	78.11	0.78	1.64	10.96	6.41	2.00	0.09
Tobacco (5)	255,249	32.97	6.68	6.92	4.12	20.12	23.72	1.99

Table 4.6 (continued)

GROUP C : Substantial Erosion of Preferences

New Potatoes (1/1 -15/5)	81,226	28.02	14.02	-	56.94	0.32	0.06	0.63
New Potatoes (16/5 - 30/6)	85,108	60.10	13.85	-	25.01	0.22	0.05	0.77
Tomatoes, fresh (1/11 - 14/5)	313,519	29.63	51.79	0.10	17.54	0.10	0.06	0.77
Sanguines and semi-sanguines (1/4 - 30/4)	5,878	13.78	42.17	-	44.18	-	-	-
Sanguines and semi-sanguines (1/5 - 15/5)	2,171	6.21	30.95	-	60.98	-	1.31	-
Sanguines and semi-sanguines (16/10 - 15/3)	28,820	38.61	17.02	-	44.01	0.29	0.07	-
Fresh Sweet Oranges: navels, navelines etc. (1/4 - 30/4)	60,752	3.54	33.21	-	62.44	0.09	0.29	0.42
Fresh Sweet Oranges: navels, navelines etc (1/5 - 15/5)	28,821	5.18	25.66	-	65.16	0.43	3.06	0.41
Fresh Sweet Oranges: navels, navelines etc. (16/10 - 15/3)	275,270	4.24	61.50	0.04	32.17	0.71	1.07	-
Fresh Sweet Oranges other than sanguines and navels, navelines etc. (16/10 - 31/3)	5,208	61.29	6.68	-	25.88	2.84	2.11	0.71
Clementines	188,956	4.14	67.54	-	28.25	0.03	0.03	-
Dried Figs	21,468	2.50	12.67	-	83.79	0.56	0.22	-
Fresh Table Grapes (15/7 - 30/10)	161,808	82.82	10.91	-	6.46	0.04	0.15	0.16
Green Beans (1/10 - 30/6)	42,881	25.95	27.81	29.44	15.17	0.69	0.86	-
Green Beans (1/7 - 30/9)	8,273	88.46	1.98	7.35	-	0.44	0.33	-
Virgin Olive Oil	66,480	13.08	60.77	-	25.91	0.06	0.18	-
Virgin Lampante Olive Oil	153,898	14.58	27.79	-	56.34	1.28	0.01	-

Table 4.6 (continued)

Capers and Olives prepared or preserved	67,891	5.20	58.74	-	35.82	0.15	0.06	-
Grape juice	57,750	82.14	9.76	-	5.92	1.12	0.81	-

(1) includes NIMEXE code numbers 2205.54 and 2205.68; includes wines of alcoholic strength 15-18% vol. other than porto, madeira, sherry and tokay.

(2) refers to NIMEXE code number 0802.37

(3) refers to the following NIMEXE numbers : 2205.21, 2205.22, 2205.31, 2205.35 and 2206.15

(4) refers to NIMEXE code numbers: 2205.29 and 2205.49 (see also note 1 above)

(5) refers to NIMEXE code numbers : 2401.15, 2401.22, 2401.34, 2401.35, 2401.36 : only tobacco varieties that are produced in the new members have been included.

Source: EUROSTAT, NIMEXE tables for the years 1979 and 1980.

CHAPTER FIVE

Prospects for the Manufacturing Exports of the Non-Candidate Mediterranean Countries in a Community of Twelve.

1 Trade Policy Changes

This chapter examines the impact of the accession of Greece, Portugal and Spain to the European Community on the exports of manufactures of the other non-member, non-candidate, Mediterranean countries. Throughout this chapter the term non-candidate Mediterranean Countries (NCMC) will be used to refer to those countries that were neither members of the EC-9 nor have yet applied for EC membership. Greece, Portugal and Spain are treated in this chapter as a group to be referred henceforth as the 'new members'.

There are at least two reasons for examining this question in some detail. First, almost all NCMC will experience trade preference erosion. These countries are selling a substantial part of their manufacturing exports to the Community of Nine under terms of market access which in some instances are better and in most cases at least equal to the market access terms offered in the pre-accession period to the three new members. Secondly, manufacturing exports have increased their importance in the structure of the total exports of the NCMC particularly over the last decade. Yugoslavia, Cyprus, Lebanon, Israel and Malta have more than 50 per cent of their exports concentrated in manufactures. Exports of manufactures account for between one-third and one half of the total exports of Tunisia, Egypt and Turkey. Morocco and Jordan have almost one quarter of their exports in manufactures and Algeria nearly one-fifth.

The effects of the second enlargement of the EC on the exports of the non-candidate countries can be examined by looking at the post-enlargement changes in terms of their market access in three separate groups of markets, namely the markets of the new members, the markets of the non-candidate countries and the markets of the EC-9.

The terms of market access of the manufacturing exports of the NCMC will be affected in several different ways. In the markets of the new members, exports from the NCMC will now enter under the same terms as in the markets of the EC-9. This will be a direct consequence of the extension to the new members of the preferential trade and cooperation agreements of the Community with the Mediterranean countries. But it must also be realised that the NCMC will be faced in the markets of the new members with positive

81

discrimination in favour of the exports from the other newly acceded countries. Before enlargement, both the NCMC and the new members exported to the markets of each candidate country under more or less the same tariff and non-tariff barriers. When the enlargement is fully completed Portuguese exports, for example, will be entering the Spanish market at more favourable terms than exports to Spain from NCMC.

In the markets of the non-candidate countries which offer reverse preferences to the Community (i.e. Turkey, Israel, Cyprus and Malta) exports from the new members will compete on preferential terms with local production and/or exports from other NCMC which are trading in those markets on most-favoured-nation conditions. This effect may apply particularly strongly on Israel whose production structure considerably overlaps the corresponding structures of the new members (for Israel see the more detailed analysis by Tovias in Gutmann, 1984).

Finally, in the markets of the EC-9 the preferences now enjoyed by the NCMC will be eroded by the removal of all tariff and non-tariff barriers on competing exports from the new members. These changes in the conditions of access into the three regional markets can be illustrated by means of the following graph.

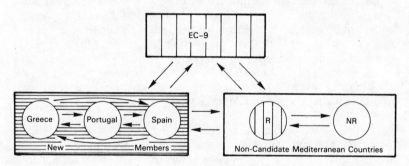

The three rectangles represent the three regional markets of the EC-9, of the new members and of the NCMC. The new members regional market is subdivided into the three national markets whilst the NCMC regional market is divided into two submarkets according to the extent that reciprocal tariff concessions are offered to the EC (submarket R) or not (submarket NR). The pointed arrows indicate the direction of trade flows. Market access conditions faced by the exports of the NCMC will be affected in the following ways :

82

(a) The three new members as a group will be placed in a more preferential position in the markets of the EC-9 in relation to the NCMC compared to the pre-enlargement period. In those product groups where preferences will be eroded trade diversion against the NCMC can potentially take place in the markets of the EC-9.

(b) In the three submarkets of the new members exports from the NCMC will be faced with lower trade (tariff and non-tariff) barriers giving rise to potential export expansion; but at the same time exports from both the EC-9 and from the other two new members will acquire an even higher preferential status and will thus be positively discriminated against exports from the NCMC.

(c) Finally, in the markets of the NCMC offering reverse preferences to the EC (submarket R in the graph) suppliers from the new members will compete on preferential terms vis-a-vis exports from the other NCMC. This also will potentially lead to trade diversion against exports from these countries.

The regional markets or submarkets where potential trade diversion effects are expected against exports from the NCMC are shaded by vertical lines. The markets shaded by horizontal lines indicate the simultaneous potential appearance of both trade expansion and trade diversion effects with an uncertain overall outcome. Only in one submarket (NR) will exports from the NCMC be free of any trade diversion effects.

2 Potential Trade Diversion Effects in the Markets of the EC-9

Let us first examine the effects of the second enlargement on the exports of the NCMC to the markets of the EC-9. How far is the preferential position of the exporters from the new members likely to cause a diversion of imports from the NCMC to the new members ? The answer to this question depends upon the following factors. First, on the degree of overlapping of the exports to the EC-9 by the three new members with the exports to the Community of Nine by the NCMC. Secondly, on the comparative conditions of entry to the EC-9 markets during the pre-enlargement period of similar products from the two groups of countries. Thirdly, on the relative competitiveness of the export supply of the two groups of countries.

Estimates of the degree of overlap between the exports of the EC-9 and the total exports of the three new members on the one hand and between the imports of the EC-9 and the exports of the three new members on the other indicate that with the exception of Greece the export structure of the new members is more similar to the export structure of the EC-9 rather than to the import structure of the

83

Community of Nine (Donges et al., 1982). This would suggest that export expansion by the new members will lead more to the displacement of less efficient local EC-9 production than to trade diversion against other importers into the Community markets. But although table 5.1 shows that the coefficients of trade conformity [1] are lower both from Spain and Portugal when their export structure is compared to the import structure of the Community than when their export structure is compared to the product composition of the exports of the EC-9, nevertheless the values of the coefficients are closer to one than to zero in both cases. This fact suggests that both trade creation within the enlarged Community and trade diversion against exporters from third countries are likely to take place.

Table 5.1: Coefficients of Conformity of Trade in Manufactures

EC-9	Year	Greece	Portugal	Spain
			Total Exports	
Total	1960	0.359	0.349	0.682
Exports	1970	0.437	0.597	0.785
	1979	0.546	0.680	0.920
			Total Exports	
Total	1960	0.384	0.392	0.769
	1970	0.666	0.729	9.898
Imports	1979	0.688	0.679	0.900
			Exports to the EC-9	
Total	1970	0.659	0.667	0.833
Imports	1979	0.618	0.606	0.865

Sources : J.B.Donges and K.W.Schatz, 1980 and J.B.Donges et al., 1982

A clearer picture emerges if instead of looking at the structure of the exports of the three new members in relation to the structure of the total imports of the EC-9 we investigate directly the structure of the exports to the Community of both sets of countries (new members and NCMC). This is done in table 5.2 which gives the values of the coefficients of trade conformity and in table 5.3 which gives the index of similarity[2] of the structure of exports to the EC-9 of both the three new members and the NCMC. The coefficients of trade conformity and the indexes of similarity were calculated for the product groups 50 to 99 of the two digit classification scheme reported in the NIMEXE tables of EUROSTAT. Tables 5.2 and 5.3 relate the export structure of each new member country to the corresponding export structure of the NCMC as a group and of three separate subregions (Maghreb, Turkey and Yugoslavia) which accounted in 1980 for about two thirds of all exports of manufactures from the Mediterranean region to the EC-9.

Table 5.2: Coefficients of Trade Conformity : Exports of Manufactures of the New Members and the Non-Candidate Mediterranean Countries to the EC-9

	Exports of the new members to the EC-9			
Exports to the EC-9 of :	Greece	Portugal	Spain	The Three
All NCMC	0.812	0.756	0.371	0.599
Yugoslavia	0.625	0.779	0.620	0.761
Turkey	0.600	0.340	0.101	0.259
Maghreb	0.695	0.651	0.145	0.363

Source : EUROSTAT, NIMEXE tables 1980

Both tables give a similar picture on the degree of overlap of trade structures. The extent of overlap between the exports of manufactures of the NCMC and those of Greece and Portugal is considerable whereas it appears to be limited as far as Spain's trade with the EC-9 is concerned. Spanish accession will thus have a relatively limited trade diversion potential against the NCMC taken as a group. When individual subregions are examined one sees that the structures of exports to the EC-9 from Yugoslavia and Spain overlap considerably. Thus Yugoslavia may experience strong diversion

85

effects against her exports to Community following the Spanish accession. Turkish exports to the Community appear to overlap relatively extensively with Greek exports to the EC-9. Generally, Greece shows the highest coefficients of trade conformity both with the NCMC as a group and with two of the regional submarkets reported in tables 5.2 and 5.3 (Turkey and Maghreb). However, Yugoslav exports of manufactures to the EC-9 have a higher index of similarity with Portuguese and Spanish exports rather than Greek.

Table 5.3: Indexes of similarity of Manufacturing Export Structures

	Exports of the new members to the EC-9			
Exports to the EC-9 of :	Greece	Portugal	Spain	The Three
All NCMC	65.24	62.06	46.19	60.54
Yugoslavia	52.20	61.73	58.65	69.65
Turkey	48.94	35.75	19.79	34.97
Maghreb	55.47	52.08	32.91	43.25

Source : EUROSTAT, NIMEXE tables 1980

3 Sensitive Products and Non-Tariff Barriers

It is now necessary to look at the similarities of export structures in terms of the degree of sensitivity of the various products in the trade policy of the EC. As is well known, certain industrial products which are defined as sensitive are subject to stricter regulations with regard to their access to the markets of the Community. Expansion of exports of such types of products by the new members will most probably be regarded as causing serious market disruption and thus invoke the application of various restraining measures on the exports of third countries. As can be seen from table 5.4 only in the category of sensitive textiles are the NCMC very important suppliers in comparison with the new members. In the other sensitive industrial products the NCMC are relatively small suppliers ; their exports to the Community in 1979 amounted to 15 per cent of the corresponding exports by the new members. A set of trade conformity coefficients and similarity indexes were calculated for the data reported in table 5.4; they appear in table 5.5 These coefficients measure the degree of overlap of export structures not by tariff heading categories (as is the case with table 5.2) but by degree of sensitivity.

86

Table 5.4: **Structure of Manufacturing Exports to the EC-9 by Degree of Sensitivity (1979)**

| | New Members | | NCMCs | |
	Value (US$mil)	per cent	Value (US$mil)	per cent
SENSITIVE				
Textiles	1599.2	16.1	1264.0	41.2
Other Industrial Products	1087.2	10.9	169.2	5.5
SEMI-SENSITIVE				
Textiles	291.4	2.9	98.0	3.2
Other Industrial Products	1790.8	18.0	397.6	12:9
NON-SENSITIVE				
Textiles	79.8	0.8	30.3	1.0
Other Industrial Products	5095.4	51.3	1105.0	36.2
Total	9943.8	100.0	3064.1	100.0

Source : EUROSTAT, NIMEXE tables 1979

The structure of exports by degree of sensitivity appears to be close between the new members and the NCMC. When exports are classified by degree of sensitivity, Greece has a highly overlapping, almost identical, structure with the NCMC. From the point of view of sensitivity to trade policy measures, Spain's export structure is overlapping to a more limited extent with the corresponding export structures of the NCMC than either Portugal's or Greece's structures of exports to the EC-9.

It is apparent from table 5.4 that the potential for trade displacement againt the NCMC will be serious particularly in the group of sensitive textiles. The heavy concentration of the manufacturing exports of the non-candidate Mediterranean countries in the group of sensitive textiles point out that export expansion by the three in this category of products is likely to result in the imposition of trade restrictions of the type used by the Community to control the flow of sensitive imports, unless the new members adopt a strategy of convergence upon the

Table 5.5: Trade Conformity and Similarity by Degree of Sensitivity

	Manufacturing Exports to the EC-9 by the New Members			
	Greece	Portugal	Spain	The Three
A. COEFFICIENTS OF TRADE CONFORMITY				
Manufacturing Exports of the NCMC	0.991	0.966	0.727	0.861
B. INDEX OF SIMILARITY				
to the EC-9	92.4	85.2	61.8	74.4

Source : EUROSTAT, NIMEXE tables, 1979

industrial structure of the Nine and cease exploiting their comparative advantage in labour intensive products (McQueen and Read, 1986a). However, the process of trade liberalisation and the increased factor mobility within the enlarged Community may encourage this process of convergence of industrial structures. Indeed Aktan's work (Aktan, 1985) suggests that the new institutional environment within which markets will operate will encourage labour intensive industries in the EC-9 and capital intensive industries in the Southern European members thereby encouraging competitive, rather than complementary structures, in the enlarged EC.

It is now important to examine the changes in the conditions of market access that enlargement will bring about for the two groups of countries. This means examining not only the size of the erosion of tariff preferences but also the extent that the new members will gain privileged access through the abolition of non-tariff barriers faced by their exports. The remaining EC tariffs are significant only on Spanish exports since Greek and Portuguese exports of manufactures have already duty free access as a result of the association and free trade agreements of the two countries with the Community. A rough estimate [3] of the size of the export expansion that is expected to result only from the elimination of the remaining EC tariffs on imports originating from the three new members is approximately US $ 359.9 mil. (at 1979 prices) of which US $ 352.9 mil. is accounted for by the

88

expansion of exports from Spain (Donges et al., 1982). Only half of this is in consumer goods of the type exported by the NCMC. This would suggest that the estimated increase of the exports of the three new members from the elimination of tariffs amounts to something equivalent to 5.5 per cent of the exports of the NCMC in 1979. It is highly unlikely that all this export expansion from the new members will be at the displacement of the exports of the NCMC to the Community. A certain part will be at the expense of inefficient Community production and a further part at the expense of exports from countries with a lower status in the preference hierarchy of the EC than the NCMC. Thus the size of the possible trade diversion effect against the NCMC will be much smaller than the figure of 5.5 per cent mentioned above. However, most of the diversion that is likely to occur will be concentrated in the field of sensitive textiles.

It is now time to recognise that for a number of product groups, particularly those under the sensitive category, preference erosion will occur mainly through the elimination of non-tariff barriers previously applicable on the trade between the EC-9 and the new members. Three types of such non-tariff barriers are worth emphasising since they are going to improve significantly the access to Community markets for the exports from the new members. These are : rules of origin, voluntary export restraints (VERs) and tariff ceilings. Rules of origin with their requirements for a minimum of local value added will no longer apply to the new members whilst they will continue to operate vis-a-vis the NCMC. This will give the exporters from the new members an additional preferential margin. VERs have been applied to many groups of textile exports of all three new members as well as on similar exports from the NCMC. Greece, for example, was (before 1981) subject to VERs on several of her textile exports to five Community countries (Belgium, France, Italy, Luxembourg and the UK). There is a danger that as the new members exercise their rights of full membership they may be tempted to seek for an extension of the coverage of the list of sensitive items in the Community's trade. Participation of the new members in the cartels operated by the Community in a few sensitive industrial products may further raise trade barriers against exports from NCMC and other third countries.

When all these changes in the terms of market access of the exports from the new members are taken into account, it is hard to deny that the size of trade preference erosion will be more than negligible. However, a loss of preferences does not necessarily imply a loss of export markets. The extent to which market shares are going to be affected depends not only on the degree of preference erosion but also on the relative competitiveness of the export supply of the country that suffers a reduction in its preference margin. Comparisons of the relative competitiveness of the export supply of the new members and the NCMC are not easy to obtain. The evolution of the revealed comparative advantages of the new members is however indicative.

The three new members are countries with strong comparative advantages mainly in labour intensive consumer goods. In the field of intermediate goods only Spain managed during the second half of the 1970s to acquire comparative advantages in fabricated metal products and in transport equipment. A study of the revealed comparative advantages of the three countries based on their export performance in the markets of the EC-9 during the period 1970-1979 (Donges et al., 1982) shows that in textiles, clothing and footwear all three countries maintained a strong competitive position. Greece and Spain showed, during the same decade, a strong competitive position in leather products and Portugal in paper and products, pottery, china and glass. In intermediate goods, the only item where all three countries obtained a high positive index of revealed comparative advantage is non-metallic minerals. Greece and Spain throughout the decade enjoyed comparative advantage in the non-ferrous metals sector, whilst Spain had a positive index of revealed comparative advantage in iron and steel products but only towards the end of the decade. In summary, the analysis of the revealed comparative advantage of the three new members shows that their competitive position is particularly strong in products which one expects to find heavily represented in the exports of countries at an early stage of their industrialisation with a few notable exceptions in the case of Spain. It appears therefore that there are not any clear signs that the three new members could not take advantage of the preferential position they will obtain after accession in the markets of the EC-9.

4 The changing position of the NCMC in the markets of the new members

Adoption of the *acquis Communautaire* by the new members clearly implies that the NCMC will eventually enjoy access conditions in the markets of the new members similar to those prevailing in the Community of the Nine. This means a reduction in the tariff and non-tariff barriers that NCMC have so far been facing in the markets of the new members. Tariffs on imports of manufactures were in the majority of the cases higher in the Three than in the Nine. For example, the range of GATT rates of customs duties was for leather products 0-40 per cent in Portugal, 0-42 per cent in Greece and 0-20 per cent in Spain but only 0-15 per cent in the EC; in footwear they ranged from 14-53 per cent in Greece and between 15 and 25 per cent in Spain but between 6 and 20 per cent in the Community. The unweighted average nominal tariff rate on imports of consumer goods from non-EC sources was almost twice as high as the corresponding level of the CET (Tovias, 1979b). Harmonisation of the tariffs of the new members to the CET will give a price advantage to the exports of the NCMC in the markets of the new members. But it should be borne in mind that the amount of trade involved is already very small. Imports of manufactures from the NCMC accounted (1977) for 1.9 per cent of Spain's manufacturing imports, 3.1 per cent of Portuguese imports of manufactures and 5.9 per cent of Greek manufacturing imports. The major exporter of manufactures to the markets of the new members is Israel - supplying about 60 per cent of the total value of manufacturing exports involved.

Adoption by the three new members of the complex network of the agreements regulating Community trade in manufactures with the developing world will place the NCMC in a more privileged position in the markets of the Three vis-a-vis other suppliers that were so far exporting to these markets on the basis of the same terms of market access as the NCMC. Thus the NCMC can take advantage in the markets of the new members not only from the trade creating effects of the downwards adjustment of the tariffs of the new members to the lower level of the CET but also from trade diverting effects against less preferred sources such as the Latin American countries or the South-East Asian ones. An additional trade discrimination effect working against the NCMC will result from the changes in the conditions of market access of the member countries in each other's market. In the pre-enlargement period the NCMC have been exporting to the individual markets of the three new members under the same conditions of market access as each individual country from the group of new members. As membership to the EC involves the extension of the customs unions to the trade among the new members, exports from the NCMC will be discriminated against exports from other countries from the new members group. There is no doubt that this new element of discrimination is bound to be produced as the logical conclusion of the extension of the customs union in the intra-trade of the new members. But the quantitative importance of this trade discrimination effect is likely to be negligible. After all, exports to Spain from Greece and Portugal amounted (1976) to 0.4 per cent of total Spanish imports. Exports to Portugal from Spain and Greece amounted to 4.8 per cent of Portuguese total imports whilst exports to Greece from the two Iberian countries were 1.5 per cent of total Greek imports. The corresponding export shares are 3.6 per cent, 2.5 per cent and 1.0 per cent respectively (Tovias, 1979b). It can however be argued that as intra-Iberian trade is stimulated from the establishment of the customs union between the two countries of the region, the

91

trade discrimination effect against NCMC may indeed become more serious than the above figures at first suggest.

5 Concluding Remarks

The above analysis indicates that the trade displacement effects of the second enlargement of the Community against the NCMC will be mainly concentrated in textiles. The textiles trade is therefore an area where trade conflicts between the enlarged EC and the NCMC can potentially arise. These trade conflicts will be added to those that will result from the extension of the Common Agricultural Policy to the new members (see chapter 4).

In some ways the trade conflicts that are now developing are a consequence of past Community policies. By concentrating its tariff and non-tariff concessions to the same groups of products, the Community encouraged their expansion throughout the Mediterranean region. As market outlets for the products to which preferences have been granted are limited, it became inevitable to have increasing quantities of citrus fruit and cotton textiles directed towards the Community markets.

The need for rectifying this state of affairs has been recently emphasised by the Commission. In a document produced in June 1982 (Commission of the European Communities, 1982a) the Commission recognises the trade conflicts that can potentially emerge from the second enlargement and proposes as a long term solution the encouragement of complementarities in the structures of agricultural and industrial production between the EC-12 and the Mediterranean region. However, developing complementarity implies agreed specialisation schemes and joint planning machinery. It is difficult to see how this will come about when neither the Community itself, nor the NCMC as a group, possess any such industrial and agricultural planning machinery within their own area. The Commission, nevertheless, proposes the setting up of a 'Mediterranean Forum'. This 'Forum' will consist of representatives from industry and agriculture interests from all countries of the EC-12 and the Mediterranean region. The principal aim of the 'Forum' will be to exchange information about future production plans and to try to forecast possible inconsistencies in investment planning decisions in an effort to reduce oversupplies or shortages. It will also provide a mechanism, an institutional framework, for an early warning on impending trade conflicts.

The Commission proposal is certainly ambitious. But this is not its defect. Any effort to promote cooperation for the benefit of all countries in the area is most welcome. But the proposal needs careful thinking otherwise it may remain stillborn like the 1972 Commission's plan for a Global Mediterranean Policy. It is perhaps for this reason that the Commission's response has subsequently shifted to a kind of conservation operation aiming at the less ambitious target of maintaining and preserving traditional flows of trade (*Europe*, No. 4132 n.s 15/16 July 1985). But even this limited action has already encountered opposition from Mediterranean member states like Greece and Italy.

Notes

1. The coefficient of trade conformity is given by the expression

$$\sum_{i=1}^{n} x_{ij}m_{ij} \, / \, \{ \sum_{i=1}^{n} x^2_{ij} \sum_{i=1}^{n} m^2_{ij} \}^{1/2}$$

where x_{ij} is the share of the exports of commodity i to country j in the total exports to country j and m_{ij} the import coefficient similarly defined. The closer to 1 this coefficient is, the higher the degree of overlap of the trade structures.

2. The similarity index is constructed as follows :

$$\sum \min (S_i \, ac \, , S_i bc \,) \times 100$$

where S = market share, i refers to product grouping, a and b are the exporting areas and c is the importing area.

This index was first used by Finger and Kreinin (1979) to assess the trade diversion effects of the GSP schemes of the major industrial countries, and subsequently by Pomfret (1981) to examine the impact of EC enlargement on NCMC's non-oil, non-manufactured exports to the European Community. Kellman and Schroder (1983) have shown that this index possesses interesting properties of stability over time but that it is sensitive to the level of commodity aggregation adopted. This is why in the exercise we supplement the analysis based on the Finger-Kreinin similarity index with the use of an alternative indicator of the degree of overlap of trade structures, namely the coefficient of trade conformity (see note 1 above). One would be on safer ground if patterns revealed through the use of the index of export similarity were confirmed by the trends in the values of the coefficient of trade conformity.

3. The estimate was derived by using the formula

$$\Delta X_i = t_i x_i \left[1 + e_{sx} (1 + t_i) \right]$$

where X = exports, t = tariff change, e_{sx} = export supply elasticity for product i.

CHAPTER SIX

Trade Effects on Third Countries from Spain's Accession to the EC

1 Trade displacement versus trade expansion

The accession of Spain to the European Community - like any extension of a customs union - will change the relative competitive position of the exports of third countries vis-a-vis Spanish exports in the markets of the enlarged Community. These relative discriminatory effects against exports from third countries are produced by the fact that exports from the new member (Spain) will enter, after the completion of accession, duty free in the markets of the EC-10 whilst exports from third countries will still have to face the tariff and other non-tariff barriers of the common external commercial policy of the EC. This relative discrimination against third country exporters will - in one sense - be more pronounced in the current phase of the enlargement of the European Community because a number of third countries are currently exporting to the EC-10 at more favourable market access conditions than Spain. Spanish entry will thus dilute some of the preferences they enjoy in the EC markets. As is well known, the Community's common external commercial policy is characterised by a hierarchical system of preferences in which some third countries, like the ACP, enjoy freer access conditions to the Community markets than others. Among the countries that used to maintain a more privileged position in comparison to Spain in the Community's hierarchy of preferences are most of the countries of the Global Mediterranean Policy. Of these countries, Turkey, Cyprus and Malta have association agreements envisaging the eventual establishment of a customs union between them and the EC, Israel has a free trade area agreement to be implemented in stages, the Maghreb and the Mashrek countries and Yugoslavia have preferential trade and cooperation agreements with the Common Market. The tariff and other concessions offered to this group of countries are by no means uniform (Mishalani et al, 1981). Even within this small regional group, some countries are more preferred than others with Yugoslavia at the bottom of the hierarchy of Mediterranean preferences. The main focus of this chapter is to assess how far the exports of this group of countries to the enlarged Community are likely to be affected from the accession of Spain to the EC.

However, it is not correct to state that the countries of the Global Mediterranean Policy will experience throughout the enlarged Community only trade discrimination effects. Again, one has to take into consideration the special circumstances of the extension of the

95

Community customs union to include Spain. This extension takes place by Spain adopting the common external tariff and the other instruments of the EC's common external commercial policy including the network of agreements making up the Global Mediterranean Policy. Given the fact that Spanish tariffs and other non-tariff barriers to trade in manufactures are higher than those of the EC this implies an action on the part of Spain almost equivalent to a unilateral tariff reduction vis-a-vis third countries - at least as far as trade in manufactures is concerned. On top of this, Spain will accede to all association, trade and cooperation agreements the Community has so far concluded with the countries of the Mediterranean region and other states. Thus in one segment of the enlarged Community market, i.e. in the Spanish market, Mediterranean exporters will experience gross trade creation effects from the realignment of Spanish tariffs and other trade policies to the Community common external commercial policy. The Spanish market of 34 million people is not an unimportant one particularly for the smaller countries of the Mediterranean region.

A tentative hypothesis to be advanced, therefore, is that following Spain's accession to the Community the countries of the Global Mediterranean Policy (GMP) will experience in the markets of EC-10 an erosion of their preferences and a possible displacement of their exports by Spanish products whilst they will enjoy beneficial gross trade creating effects in the Spanish market from the alignment of Spain's tariff structure to that of the Community. This last part of the hypothesis must be qualified as far as most agricultural products are concerned given the prohibitive trade barriers operated within the Community particularly on imports of temperate zone and several Mediterranean types of produce like wine (see chapter 4).

2 Indicators of export expansion potential

Let us look first at the potential expansion (gross trade creation) of the exports of the countries of the GMP. One interesting indicator of this potential is the difference between the Community and Spain in their share of imports originating from developing countries. One would expect that if tariff preferences conferred competitive advantages then the countries with preferential trade arrangements with the Community would have, other things being equal (i.e. income levels and tastes), a higher share in the imports of the EC than in the imports of Spain. When total imports (excluding minerals and fuels i.e commodities for which tariff preferences have no practical meaning) are taken into account (see table 6.1), it appears that the share of developing countries is actually higher in the imports of Spain (which offers no preferential trade concessions to LDCs) than in the imports of the Community. This difference is however due entirely to the fact that

96

Spain imports a relatively larger share of her agricultural imports from the developing countries compared to the EC. When agricultural products are excluded both from the Spanish and the Community imports then the picture changes. The Community, which concentrates in any case its tariff preferences principally to manufactures, imports a larger share of manufacturing goods from LDCs than Spain does. Given the differences in income per capita levels and in tastes between Spain and the Community it is more advisable to compare not total Community shares but rather the shares of Community countries with similar income per capita levels and tastes to the corresponding Spanish shares. Table 6.2 makes this comparison by choosing Italy - a Mediterranean country, with income per capita levels and production structures closer to Spain's than other EC countries. In Italy, an original member of the Community, which has long adapted to the Community system of preferential trading with selected groups of LDCs, the developing countries enjoy a share in its imports of manufactures twice as high as that of Spain. The difference between the two shares can be taken as an indicator of the potential export expansion that these countries can experience when Spain adopts the preferential trading system with the LDCs followed by the Community.

Focusing specifically on the share of the countries of the GMP in the imports of the Community and Spain (table 6.1), one observes that these countries contribute twice as large a share in the imports of the Community as they do in the case of Spain. This holds both for agricultural and manufacturing products. The difference in the import shares between the EC and Spain from the countries of the GMP indicates the approximate expansion to be experienced in the Spanish markets by Mediterranean exporters[1] but does not certainly suggest that the two shares would equalise. Dissimilarities of the structures of comparative advantage between EC and Spain would preclude this.

The weak trading links of Spain with the countries of the GMP are also seen from the share of these countries in the Spanish imports from LDCs compared to the corresponding shares of the Community (table 6.3). Approximately 7 per cent of EC imports from developing countries originate from the countries of the GMP compared to 2.6 per cent of Spanish imports from developing countries. Regarding manufacturing imports, the share of the Community's imports from LDCs originating from the countries of the GMP is higher (7.4 per cent) than the corresponding share of Spain's imports from LDCs (5.2 per cent).

97

Table 6.1: Shares (percentages) of Selected Groups of Countries in the Imports of the EC and Spain (averages 1978-79)

Import Category	Shares of Developing Countries in Imports of :		Shares of Countries of GMP in Imports of :	
	EC	Spain	EC	Spain
All Imports (except SITC 2 and 3)	13.5	16.4	0.95	0.43
Agricultural Products	30.0	52.4	1.93	0.81
Manufacturing Products	9.8	6.2	0.73	0.32

Source : OECD Statistics of Foreign Trade, Series C

Table 6.2: Share of Developing Countries (percentages) in the Manufacturing Imports of Italy and Spain (averages 1978-79)

SITC	ITALY	SPAIN
5	7.1	7.7
6	20.0	10.8
7	5.3	1.9
8	14.4	10.2
Total	13.5	6.2

Source : OECD Statistics of Foreign Trade, Series C

The preferential treatment of the Mediterranean exports in the markets of Spain following the adoption of the *acquis communautaire* by the new member would lead to the displacement of certain groups of developing countries' exporters by the preferred sources from the Mediterranean[2]. This displacement of traditional exporters to the Spanish market by preferred producers from the countries of the GMP will be strong in the cases where the introduction of the EC preferential trade agreements is not to be accompanied by a general reduction in the trade barriers. This is going to be the case in the majority of agricultural products. To see which groups of countries are likely to suffer most from potential trade displacement effects we calculated the Finger-Kreinin similarity indices between the structure of exports to Spain of the countries of the GMP and the structure of exports to Spain of two groups of developing countries : Non-OECD America and South-East Asia. The values of the similarity indexes (table 6.4) indicate that the countries of Non-OECD America are more likely to experience this trade displacement particularly in manufacturing products; in the case of agricultural products the similarity between the two groups of countries is approximately the same. In both cases however the values of the similarity index are small.

Table 6.3: Share of the countries of the GMP in imports from developing countries (averages 1978-79)

	EC	SPAIN
Total Imports	7.0	2.6
Agricultural Imports	6.4	1.5
Manufacturing Imports	7.4	5.2

Source : OECD Statistics of Foreign Trade, Series C

Table 6.4: Similarity of the structure of exports to Spain of the countries of the GMP with selected groups of countries (average 1978-79; percentages)

	Non-OECD America	South-East Asia
Agricultural Exports to Spain	21.8	24.7
Manufacturing Exports to Spain	37.2	24.5

Source : OECD Statistics of Foreign Trade, Series C

99

3 The determinants of trade displacement

We now turn our attention to the EC-10 markets and ask ourselves how extensive is likely to be the dilution of preferences so far enjoyed by the countries of the GMP in these markets.   There are four main factors that will determine how serious will be the impact of preference erosion on Mediterranean exports.   The first factor is the degree of overlap of Mediterranean exports of manufactures with the manufacturing exports from Spain to the EC.   The second factor is the price responsiveness of Spain's export supply.   The third factor is the competitiveness of the export supply of the countries of the GMP or more precisely their cost advantage in relation to the size of the preference loss.   Finally, given the Community's system of preferences hierarchy, the proportion of the Community import markets supplied by less preferred countries will determine the extent to which the expansion of exports from Spain will be at the expense of the countries of the GMP or less preferred sources.   The countries of the GMP may experience a preference loss but if they are still preferred vis-a-vis other regional groups, it is upon these groups that the trade displacement effect will fall.

The composition of the exports of Spain and of the countries of the GMP to the EC is given in table 6.5.   There are some characteristic differences in the composition of the exports to the EC of these two groups.   The Mediterranean countries concentrate a larger proportion of their exports to the Community than Spain in agricultural products and in the manufacturing products of SITC 6 and 8 (semi-processed goods, textiles, clothing and similar).

To evaluate more accurately the degree of overlap between the exports of the two groups of countries we used trade data at the three digit level to calculate the Finger-Kreinin similarity index.   The values of the index at this level of aggregation are fairly low for manufacturing exports indicating a very limited potential of trade displacement from preference erosion (table 6.6) but considerably higher for agricultural trade suggesting serious trade displacement effects.

This evidence should not surprise us. The Spanish economy has now reached a level of industrial development that has led to important changes in the product composition of her manufacturing exports. These changes in the structure of the manufacturing exports make Spanish exports more directly competitive with domestic production in the European Community rather than with the manufacturing exports originating from the countries of the GMP.

100

Table 6.5 : Composition of Exports of Spain and the countries of the GMP to the EC (average 1978-79; percentages)

Commodity Group	Spanish Exports	Exports from countries of GMP
SITC 0	22.2	33.4
SITC 1	3.2	1.5
SITC 4	0.6	2.3
SITC 5	5.2	8.8
SITC 6	26.5	23.7
SITC 7	30.5	7.5
SITC 8	11.8	22.8
	100.0	100.0

Source : OECD, Statistics of Foreign Trade - Series C

Table 6.6 : Similarity Indexes : exports of Spain and the Countries of the GMP to the European Community

	(percentages)
Agricultural Exports	76.5
Manufacturing Exports	26.8

Given that several Mediterranean type of agricultural products are price sensitive, the loss of the preference margin enjoyed by some Mediterranean exporters combined with the high degree of overlap of their exports with those from Spain will lead to a loss in market shares. Morocco, Algeria, Israel, Tunisia and Cyprus used to enjoy a margin of preference vis-a-vis the weighted average EC tariff rates imposed on the same agricultural products from Spain ranging between 4 and 12 per cent (see chapter 4).

The Finger-Kreinin similarity index is sensitive to the degree of aggregation used (Kellman and Schroder, 1983). For this reason, we calculated for specific groups of products separate indices utilising a finer level of aggregation. From the various groups of agricultural products we selected fruit and vegetables (SITC 05) and beverages (SITC 11) and from the groups of manufacturing products, textiles (SITC 65), and clothing (SITC 84). The values of the similarity index for this disaggregated set of products appear in table 6.7.

101

Table 6.7 : Similarity Indexes for selected groups of exports of Spain and the countries of the GMP to the European Community

	(percentages)
Fruit and Vegetables	84.6
Beverages	99.6
Textiles	49.8
Clothing	66.2

The calculations shown in table 6.7 confirm the high degree of similarity of agricultural exports to the EC from the countries of the GMP and Spain but reveal that for certain groups of manufacturing exports the potential trade displacement effect can be as high as in the trade in agricultural products.

The high degree of similarity in the export structure does not mean that when trade preferences are eroded trade displacement against the countries whose preference margin is reduced will definitely take place (Kreinin, 1974).

4 Response to tariff preferences

For trade displacement to take place the loss of the preference margin and the similarity of export structures are necessary but not sufficient conditions. The emerging market opportunity for the new preferred partner (i.e. the new Community member) will be captured only to the extent that the domestic supply conditions are elastic enough to ensure a high production repsonse to changes in the prices enjoyed by producers. In this context it is useful to look into two indicators : first, the proportion of Spain's trade already directed to the EC and secondly, the evidence on how Spanish producers have responded so far to the limited tariff preferences they enjoyed on the basis of the 1970 trade agreement with the EC.

From the data of table 6.8 it can be seen that already a large share of Spanish exports, particularly in products where the value of the similarity index is high is directed to the EC. There are thus limits to the export diversion that may be practised by Spanish producers wishing to take advantage of the new preferential margin to be enjoyed vis-a-vis exporters from the countries of the GMP.

Table 6.8 : Share of Spanish exports directed to the EC (average 1978-79)

SITC	Percentage of World Exports	Percentage of Exports to OECD
0	61.7	72.6
1	53.8	65.0
4	24.6	41.0
5	36.5	59.7
6	38.5	71.9
7	52.7	82.0
8	45.1	59.8
Total of above	46.1	71.8

Source : OECD Statistics of Foreign Trade-Series C

An analysis of the record of Spanish exports between 1974 (the first year after the first enlargement of the Community) and 1979 shows that after standardising for differences in the rates of income growth of the importing area and for changes in the relative competitive position of Spain, the residual element in export trade growth is of modest size indicating a limited response to the tariff preferences granted to Spanish exporters in the EC markets from the 1970 trade treaty. As this trade treaty between EC and Spain offered tariff preferences only for manufactures, the analysis of trade performance is concentrated in the field of manufacturing trade only. To standardise for changes in the relative competitive position and for EC income growth we compared the export performance (annual rates of growth of exports) of Spain to that of two countries with a more limited preferential treatment in the markets of the Community. The choice of the countries selected is obviously important and for this reason we selected one country from Southern Europe, namely Yugoslavia, and one from Latin America, namely Brazil. The results of the exercise, demonstrate a modest gross trade creating effect produced by the presence of preferences in favour of Spain. The fact that the overall ratio (table 6.9) is only marginally above one (1), certainly indicates a rather modest impact of the preferences on trade flows but it may be argued that the uncertainty regarding the permanence of the tariff advantages offered could have restrained the Spanish producers from responding more vigorously to the tariff preferences offered. EC membership, by removing this uncertainty, could produce a more substantial export thrust by Spain's producers.

103

Table 6.9: Comparison of export trade performance (annual average growth rates of exports) 1974-79

Exporting Country	Importing Area	
	EC	Other OECD
Spain	39.8	15.0
Yugoslavia	12.8	5.6
Brazil	38.0	27.1

The overall ratios after standardising for income growth and relative competitive changes are 1.16 when Spain is compared to Yugoslavia and 1.90 when compared to Brazil. This evidence indicates that the supply response to tariff preferences has so far been modest and therefore suggests that the potential trade displacement effects will only incompletely materialise.

5 Mediterranean exports in Community imports

Finally, it is worth looking at another issue raised earlier, namely the extent to which in the product groups with a high degree of trade overlap between Spain and the countries of the GMP, the non-preferred sources in the tariff hierarchy of the EC are still suppliers of some significance. If this happens to be the case, then any export thrust by Spain will be primarily at the expense of these suppliers rather than suppliers from the still preferred sources in the Mediterranean. As non-preferred sources we take the non-European developed market economies. As can be seen from table 6.10 for the products of export interest to the countries of the GMP (e.g. inorganic chemicals, leather products, wood and cork, non-metallic manufactures, non-ferrous metals and clothing) the present market share of these countries does not appear to be threatened even if Spain doubles its current share due to a strong response to the competitive advantage gained through the preferential status to be enjoyed under conditions of full membership. For example, Spain accounted for 0.7 per cent of the EC imports of inorganic chemicals compared to a share of 2.6 per cent accounted by the GMP countries. Any Spanish export thrust that may materialise here is likely to be at the expense of the non-preferred suppliers from the group of the non-European Developed Countries which accounted for 17.2 per cent of the import market of the EC in these products. The **only** exception appears to

Table 6.10: Share of Non-European Developed Economies, Spain and the countries of the GMP in the EC imports of manufactures (average, 1978-79)

SITC		Non-European Developed Countries	Spain	Countries of the GMP
52	Inorganic chemicals	17.2	0.7	2.6
61	Leather products	3.1	5.4	3.6
62	Rubber products	7.0	4.7	0.6
63	Wood and Cork	9.5	2.8	3.2
64	Paper Products	9.8	1.0	0.03
65	Textiles and Yarns	5.9	1.4	1.7
66	Non-metallic manufactures	5.4	0.9	2.5
67	Iron and Steel	3.8	3.6	0.1
68	Non-ferrous metals	11.6	0.9	8.6
84	Clothing	2.1	1.2	4.6
85	Footwear	0.6	6.5	0.7

Source : OECD Statistics of Foreign Trade - Series C

be the group of leather products. In order to isolate other possible cases of serious trade displacement effects, we report below the analysis of the market shares of two product groups (65 and 84) but at the three digit level of SITC. This additional analysis reveals a few more cases of potential trade displacement against the countries of the GMP - i.e. SITC sections 655, 842, 846 and 848 (table 6.11).

The upshot of this analysis is that the erosion of the preferences granted to the countries of the GMP could lead to sizeable trade displacement effects whose importance increases by the fact that they will be concentrated in a few product groups i.e. fruit and particularly citrus fruit, beverages and especially wine, leather goods and several products from the clothing group.

Table 6.11 : Geographical Origin of Selected Community Imports (percentages, average for 1978-79)

SITC Section	Non-European Developed Countries	Spain	GMP Countries
651 : Textile Yarn	6.7	2.0	1.5
652 : Cotton Fabrics, woven	11.2	0.5	2.2
653 : Fabrics woven, of man-made fibres	8.5	1.3	0.3
655 : Knitted or crocheted fabrics	3.8	3.3	0.8
657 : Special textile fabrics and related products	8.7	1.3	1.1
658 : Made-up articles wholly/ chiefly of textile materials	5.0	1.7	2.3
659 : Floor coverings etc.,	1.4	0.2	3.9
842 : Men's outer garments of textile fabrics	3.4	2.1	7.2
843 : Women's outer garments of textile fabrics	0.5	0.3	3.8
845 : Knitted outer garments	1.1	0.5	3.7
846 : Knitted or crocheted under garments	1.8	2.0	5.0
848 : Articles of apparel and clothing accessories, no textiles	4.5	3.1	2.4

Source : OECD Statistics of Foreign Trade - Series C

However, these potential losses of market shares in Community imports must be properly compared with the expected benefits from export expansion in the Spanish market. We have seen that both the countries of the GMP and other LDCs benefiting from Community preferences can expect to raise their shares in the Spanish market once the new member aligns its tariff structure to the CET and adopts the preferential trade accords of the EC. However, one should look not only at the size of the aggregate trade displacement effects but also at their distribution among the various countries of the GMP. It appears that the burden from trade displacement effects will be felt more strongly by some countries. For example, in the case of EC Mediterranean fruit trade one sees that certain countries of the area rely on the EC markets almost exclusively for the sale abroad of their produce. In 1982-1983, 100 per cent of Tunisia's exports of oranges, 78.6 per cent of Cyprus's, 64.1 per cent of Morocco's and 62.6 per cent of Israel's exports of oranges were sold to the

106

Community compared to 5.6 per cent for Turkey or 4.9 per cent for Egypt.

One issue not discussed so far is the preferential margin that Spanish exports will acquire vis-a-vis GMP exporters (a) in Portugal and (b) in the countries of the region offering reciprocal tariff concessions to the EC (Turkey, Israel, Cyprus and Malta). There will certainly be a preference gain here for Spain and a potential displacement of trade from the countries of the GMP. However, the quantitative importance of this development is going to be small given the weak trading links among the Mediterranean countries themselves (Tovias, 1979b).

6 Concluding Remarks

Strong evidence for potential trade displacement effects against the exports of the GMP countries from Spain's accession to the EC was found by analysing the similarity of their export structures and the composition of EC imports by level of preferences granted. The question that remains to be raised is the extent to which these potential trade displacement effects will acutally materialise in practice. For this will depend, *inter alia*, on the supply responsiveness of both indigenous, Spanish, firms and 'footloose' international production to the changes in cost competitiveness caused by adjustments in tariff structures. Changes in tariff structures can indeed generate sufficiently large improvements in cost competitiveness (Johnson, 1967). How far these improvements will lead to changes in trade flows depends on the structural characteristics of the benefiting industries that determine their ability to expand production in response to changes in tariff structures. A study of the determinants of supply elasticities in individual Spanish industries is beyond the scope of this chapter. However, as we have seen in section 4, the study of the response of the Spanish manufacturing industry to the preferences granted to it in the EC markets from the 1970 trade treaty suggests that the extent to which Spanish exports will displace exports from GMP countries may be limited in practice.

This tentative conclusion must be subject to two qualifications. First, unlike most of the 1970s when the Spanish economy was near a full employment level Spain in the 1980s is characterised by high levels of unemployment and thus with plentiful supplies of unskilled and semi-skilled labour. It is this type of labour that is most relevant for a potential export thrust of the sectors likely to improve their cost competitiveness from the changes in tariff structures. Equally important in this context is the fact that real wages have actually fallen over the past two years (1984-1985). Secondly, under a preferential

107

trade agreement of temporary duration and limited product coverage, uncertainty concerning these tariff preferences may have limited their impact. Spain's new status as a full member of the EC will remove such uncertainty and could thus lead to a larger supply response than that recorded during the period the preferential trade treaty was in operation.

It is also worth noting that the products likely to gain in cost competitiveness from the realignment of tariffs are goods produced by industries with a 'footloose' locational orientation. Improved cost competitiveness in the post-accession period from Spanish locations may induce international firms to switch production there from other locations-particularly from outside the enlarged EC. As already mentioned changes in tariff structures are likely to induce responses not only from indigenous firms but, perhaps more so, from multinational firms. Given Spain's current high rating by foreign investors such response should not be underestimated. Recent trends in foreign direct investment flows to Spain suggest that the country continues to remain a favoured location for multinational production. According to the data of the General Secretariat of External Transactions of the Spanish Ministry of Commerce and Tourism foreign direct investment in Spain has risen from 85,415 million pesetas in 1980 and 78,604 million pesetas in 1981 to 188,842 and 158,180 million pesetas for 1982 and 1983 respectively. Credit ratings for Spain provided by international banking institutions seem to confirm this view.

Regarding indigenous firms, some doubts must be expressed as to the strength of their potential for expansion to service export markets. Some of the structural weaknesses of the Spanish industry (sub-optimal plant sizes, use of outmoded equipment, undercapitalisation, neglect of R & D etc.,) will act as serious constraining factors (Donges and Schatz, 1985). Also important in this respect is the neglect of modernisation of the capital stock of the Spanish industry. During the period 1980-1984 the gross equipment investment ratio fell to an annual average of 6.5 per cent from a level of 9.0 per cent in 1970-1974. (The corresponding figures for the gross total investment ratio are 19.2 per cent and 23.0 per cent respectively). This weak investment performance is bound to constrain the future supply responsiveness of the Spanish industry to the more favourable conditions brought about by the realignment of the country's tariff structure.

The reservations regarding the expected size of the trade displacement effects from Spain's accession to the EC do not necessarily apply to agriculture. As the experiences of Ireland in the 1970s and of Greece

108

in the 1980s have demonstrated the production response from the application of the Common Agricultural Policy in low income/low price economies could be substantial.

Notes

(1)   Given the strong traditional links of Spain with the Latin American countries it is interesting to compare the GMP countries experience with the impact on Latin American exports from improved market access conditions to Spain following the adoption of the GSP and the lowering of certain external tariffs, particularly on manufactures.   The UN Economic Commission for Latin America (ECLA, 1981) estimated that the trade that will experience improved market access conditions accounts for 8.8. per cent of Spain's imports from Latin America in 1979.   About two thirds of this (i.e. $126.4 million in 1979) results from the adoption of the GSP by Spain.   Of course, as a result of its accession to the EC, Spain will raise its tariff and non-tariff barriers on several imported goods from third countries. This will be particularly the case in agricultural trade.   Thus the trade from Latin America favourably affected from Spanish membership of the EC must be compared with the trade that will experience increased tariff and non-tariff barriers in the Spanish market.   The same ECLA (1981) study estimates that the increase in tariff and non-tariff barriers, particularly on CAP products, will affect 36.6 per cent of Spanish imports from Latin America (or $828.8 million in 1979).

(2)   Of course, similar trade displacement effects will be experienced by other Third World regions.   For example, for Latin America countries trade worth $753.1 million in 1977 is expected to experience preference erosion effects in the markets of EC-9 as a result of the improved access of Spain to these markets.   This trade represents approximately 6 per cent of total EC-9 imports from Latin America (ECLA, 1981).   At the same time, improved access by EC-9 in the Spanish markets will adversely affect another part of the Latin American trade with the enlarged EC.   This is estimated (ECLA,1981) to be a small proportion of Spain's imports from Latin America (4.2 per cent or $66.5 million in 1977) gives the low degree of similarity of the two export trade structures.   The final picture of trade expansion and trade displacement effects that emerges from the ECLA study is given in table 6.12.

Table 6.12: Trade Expansion and Trade Displacement Effects on Latin America

Total Imports	Spanish Imports from L.A (million US$)	Share of total Spanish Imports from L.A. %	EC-9 Imports from L.A. (million US$)	Share of E.C.-9 from L.A. %
Potential Trade Expansion Effects				
- from external tariff reductions	71.9[a]	3.2[a]	-	-
- from adoption of the GSP	126.4[a]	5.6[a]	-	-
Potential Trade Displacement Effects				
- from increases in external tariff and non-tariff barriers	828.8[a]	36.6[a]	-	-
- from improved EC-9 access to Spain	66.5[b]	4.2[b]	-	-
- from improved Spanish access to EC-9	-	-	753.1[b]	5.9[b]

(a)   refers to 1979

(b)   refers to 1977

Source:	UN Commission for Latin America, Las Relaciones Económicas entre España e Iberoamérica, Santiago de Chile, 1981.

110

CHAPTER SEVEN

The Trade Interests of the United States and the Enlargement of the EC

1 Introduction

Ambivalence and asymmetry have become the characteristic hallmarks of the economic relations between the US and the EC. Political and strategic considerations encourage the United States to support moves towards political integration in Europe. A strong ally across the Atlantic helps towards the attainment of the objectives of the United States policy to contain the Soviet Union. American endorsement of the moves for political integration in Western Europe has been constantly given from the time of the launching of the Community of the Six up to the most recent Iberian enlargement.

Indicative of this consistency in the policy of the United States towards European integration is the statement made by the delegation of the American Congress at the end of the 24th six-monthly meeting of delegations from the European Parliament and the US Congress. Congressman T. Lantos, joint chairman of the meeting, declared that the American Congress was in principle very much in favour of Community enlargement to Spain and Portugal because, as he put it "the consolidation of democracy in Europe must by far override the economic implications which the enlargement will not fail to have for the United States" (*Europe*, No. 4003, New Series, 10 January 1985). Other observers (Tovias, 1986) noted that the United States fully realised that Spanish accession to the EC could positively contribute to raise the support for continued membership of NATO - a factor of considerable importance given the decision of the PSOE to put Spain's membership of NATO to a referendum.

However, to obtain the benefit from European political integration the United States has had to pay an economic price - the price of being relatively discriminated in the markets of the Community with the concomitant loss of export trade. As the US is placed at the bottom of the EC's hierarchy of preferences, American exporters have felt over the years the impact of the relative trade discrimination effects of the formation and the geographical extensions of the European customs unions. This treatment of the US exports in the markets of the EC adds a dimension of asymmetry in the commercial relations between the US and the EC. For, whilst the EC places imports from the US at the bottom of its hierarchy of preferences, the US treats imports from the EC on an equal basis with imports from other parts of the world with the exception of the limited quantities of imports under the GSP.

111

The economic price a nation is prepared to pay for the attainment of foreign policy goals depends on how that nation perceives the value of the political benefits it gains in relation to the size of the economic costs it has to incur. In the case of the EC-US relations, the political gains have fallen below original American expectations whilst the economic losses have become progressively more harmful. Political integration in Western Europe has proceeded at a slower pace than originally envisaged. A loose framework of political cooperation and lack of defence cooperation have not helped Europe to become the strong political ally the US wanted. The EC has remained a civilian power of limited effectiveness in world affairs. Furthermore, as the global interests have steadily shifted towards the Pacific basin the perceived value of the benefits from a strong and united Europe have diminished in relative importance. The net economic costs from the relative discrimination of US exports appear to have risen with the successive geographical extensions of the EC. At the time of the formation of the EC-6, external trade creation far outweighed trade diversion. Indeed the net economic impact of the formation of the EC-6 on US trade has been favourable (table 7.1). The first enlargement produced a zero net effect. However, the second enlargement is expected to generate an adverse net effect on US trade - although in absolute terms it is of moderate size. However, this net diversionary effect on US exports materialises at a time of considerable strain on the American balance of payments.

In addition, the EC's policy of preferential trading with a number of the Mediterranean countries became another source of diversionary effects on US exports.

With the cost, in terms of trade diversion and exclusion from the EC markets, becoming more visible and the actual political gains falling below expectations, the US attitude towards European integration has been shifting steadily from encouraging to critical (Wallace, 1982).

The growing uneasiness of the US is also related to the heavy concentration of the trade diversion (and/or trade destruction) effects on a few items of sensitive exports. In its policy towards the EC, the US Administration has not been merely concerned with the overall balance of trade creation and trade diversion effects from the formation and enlargement of the European customs union. Its policy has been directed persistently towards the minimisation of the trade diversion effects irrespective of the size of the external trade creation effects of the EC. This tendency was strengthened by the fact that most of the trade diversion effects of the formation and extension of the EC were concentrated in agricultural trade - a section of trade inextricably linked with critical issues of American domestic politics. The reason for this concentration of the trade diversion effects on a limited range of agricultural products is of course linked to the international implications of the Common Agricultural Policy.

2 Background to the disputes of the 1980s

Agricultural products have featured prominently in the trade disputes between the US and the EC since the formative years of the Community. The introduction at the end of 1962 of the EC levy on the transformation products of cereals led to a sharp drop of the Community's imports of poultry meat. Poultry meat imports into the EC dropped from $52 million in 1962 to $21 million in 1966. In the case of the transformation products the import levy contained a fixed component which amounted to a duty on the value added in the production of the broiler. This duty, when fixed in 1962, was highly protective because the cost of transforming grain into broilers was much higher in the EC (where the new techniques of industrial production of broilers were at their early stage of adoption) than in the US (Fauvel, 1971). This led to a serious setback to American exports of poultry meat to the EC and eventually to American retaliation in 1963 with the imposition of a duty on imports of cognac from the EC. Thus, the first serious trade dispute between the US and the EC coincided with the launching of the CAP.

American perceptions about the significance of the CAP for US agricultural trade have changed with the changing fortunes of the US trade balance. At the time of the inception of the CAP and indeed a few years before the 'chicken war', US policy appeared to underestimate the potential impact of the CAP to the extent that the US Administration has not taken up the offer made by the Community in the early 1960s to bind support levels and to set a 90 per cent upper limit on EC self-sufficiency in grains (Tangermann, 1984). When, later in the same decade, the US exports were experiencing difficulties for a variety of reasons, removing market protection in the EC became again the main focus of US efforts to stimulate additional sales of American farm products (Paarlberg, 1984). The 1973 Flanagan report prepared by the US Department of Agriculture for the US Senate summarised in an alarmist mood the serious consequences of the CAP particularly on US feedgrain exports. But subsequent events in the world economy (devaluation of the dollar, the opening of the Soviet Union market etc.) reversed this trend and with it the interest of the US in CAP reform. As a result US pressure for liberalising agricultural trade in the framework of the GATT Tokyo Round has diminished. In fact the 'turkey war' that erupted in 1976 for reasons similar to those that produced the 'chicken war' led eventually to mutual concessions and to a US tacit aknowledgement that the

113

machinery of the CAP was in line with the spirit if not the letter of the GATT. Furthermore, in 1979 the EC's mechanism of export refunds was endorsed as in line with GATT practices in agricultural trade.

Despite the substantial growth of US exports of agricultural exports to the EC which rose from $7,700 million in 1971 to $41,000 million in 1980 the American concern shifted in the 1980s to the challenge posed by the Community in third markets.

However, US concern with the challenge posed by EC policies for American trade interests in third countries goes back to the late 1960s. The policy of the EC to enter into preferential trading arrangements with selected groups of developing countries has created opposition in the United States both because it ran contrary to the principle of multilateralism upon which the GATT edifice was built and because it endangered the position of US exporters in the markets of the EC's privileged partners (Robertson, 1976). Particularly strong was the US reaction to the preferential trade agreements negotiated between the EC and most of the countries of the Mediterranean region. Preferential trade arrangements with the Yaoundé group did not raise strong opposition as they essentially represented a continuation of the preexisting colonial ties. The Mediterranean agreements represented in most cases an extension of such practices to countries in the Mediterranean basin with no colonial trading ties with the EC's founding members. Furthermore, the Mediterranean agreements involved reciprocal tariff concessions (reverse preferences). This means that US export trade interests were threatened in the markets of both the EC-6 and the Mediterranean associated countries.

Subsequently, and under the threat that the US will not offer GSP treatment to LDCs that extend reciprocal tariff concessions to the EC, most of the Mediterranean agreements were renegotiated in the early 1970s to become simple development cooperation agreements with no reciprocity. On the basis of estimates of elasticities of substitution ranging from 2 for the medium-run to 3.5-4.0 for the long-run, Kreinin (1976) estimated that the value of US exports of manufactures likely to be displaced in the markets of the Mediterranean region offering reverse preferences to the EC ranged from the $137 million (at 1969 prices) for the medium-run (i.e. after a period of adjustment extending over 4 years) to $275 for the longer-run. A product by product analysis by the US Department of State estimated the US export loss in the associated Mediterranean countries other than Greece and Turkey to $140 million for 1969. This represented 0.7 per cent of the 1969 US exports. The smallness of this estimate supports the view that the attitude of the US towards the EC's policy of preferential trading arrangements with the Mediterranean countries was based on general principles rather than on direct commercial interest. However, the concentration of the export losses from the EC's preferential trading in particular products and exporting regions had given a disproportionate political dimension to this trade conflict. This has been particularly noticeable in the US reaction to export losses from direct preferences in the EC markets in favour of Mediterranean exporters especially of citrus fruit. Citrus fruit exports from the associated Mediterranean countries are given favourable market access conditions (lower customs duties) placing exports of US citrus fruit at a relative disadvantage in the EC markets. Despite the fact that most of the Mediterranean agreements ceased to involve reciprocal preferences and became straightforward development cooperation treaties, the US Administration, under the impact of politically powerful farm lobbies, continued to insist that American exporters of citrus fruit products be given the same treatment as those of a number of Mediterranean countries. The long history of the cartelisation of the California-Arizona orange industry (Shepard, 1986) explains to a considerable extent the influence it exerts on commercial policy making in the United States. The US brought this dispute to the GATT. Eventually, a disputes panel ruled that the EC's preferential arrangements for Mediterranean citrus fruit producers hurt American interests and recommended compensation. However, at the GATT council the panel report was not accepted, as action by the council requires unanimity. The Commission explained its blocking of the endorsement of the GATT panel recommendation by pointing to the broader objectives of the EC's Mediterranean policy. "The United States does not understand, does not grasp the geo-political dimension of our preferential agreements with the Mediterranean countries" stated Commissioner Andriessen (*Europe*, Friday 12 July 1985), adding that "we cannot allow this policy to be brought into question by a GATT panel".

In an effort to force the EC to allow more US citrus fruit into the Community the US government had threatened to raise pasta tariffs by up to 40 per cent in retaliation. The US action could have affected $36 million of EC pasta exports - $35 million worth from Italy. The choice of pasta as the product to retaliate was not random. The US decided to hit the EC on a product it has had trouble with in the past. In 1983 a GATT panel upheld a US complaint that the EC pasta exports were unfairly subsidised, but the panel report was not endorsed by the GATT council because of the unanimity rule.

Within a week of the decision of the Reagan Administration to retaliate, the Commission of the EC suggested to the Council to respond by proposing to raise the EC tariff on nuts in shells and lemons from 8 per cent to 30 per cent. Sales of US nuts in shells and

115

lemons to the EC were then worth $33 million. This citrus and pasta trade war was quickly terminated indicating perhaps that the speedy counter-action of the EC to the US threat of retaliation paved the way for a quick resolution of the dispute. The settlement of this trade dispute has not effectively upset the EC's policy of giving Mediterranean citrus producers preferential access to the Community market. The EC settled this dispute by reducing its export subsidies over pasta sold to the US from ECU 14 to ECU 8 per 100 kgs. The main implication of this settlement is that it has left intact the EC's defence of the principle that it may use export subsidies for processed foods.

European attempts to tackle the growing agricultural surpluses of the Community have opened additional sources of conflicts with the US. The disposal in outside markets at subsidised prices of the ever increasing European surpluses has intensified the competition that American exports meet in third markets. The US regards this as unfair competition and for this reason it filed in 1981 complaints with GATT concerning Community export refunds on sugar, poultrymeat and wheat flour. When the US failed to win these cases in the GATT council it started in 1983 its own system of export aids. The US Bonus Incentive Commodity Export Programme (BICEP) started with $2,000 million behind it to help American farmers to capture (or recapture) markets held by the EC. This time, it was the Community that decided to file a complaint with GATT (Green Europe, 1984a). This hidden trade war of the early 1980s moved closer to an open trade war in the mid-1980s following the conclusion of the negotiations for the entry of Portugal and Spain in the EC.

3 The Trade Dispute from the Second Enlargement

The implications of the second enlargement of the EC on the economic interests of the US extend beyond agricultural trade. The liberalisation of trade between the EC-9 and the new members and the adoption by the latter of the CET and the other trade policy instruments of the Community's network of external commercial relations will affect both manufacturing and agricultural trade between the EC and the United States.

First, US manufacturing exports to the EC-9 are likely to be displaced by similar exports from the new members. The new members now enjoy a margin of preference compared to non-members and this enables them to displace competitive imports from countries such as the United States. The size of this trade diversion effect depends, *inter alia*, on the elasticity of substitution between preferred new member and non-preferred US suppliers. The exact degree of substitutability between these two sources of supply is not known. Indirect estimates by Sawyer (1984) and Pomfret (1985) give values of the expected trade diversion against US exports of manufactures to the EC-9 ranging from $1.4 million to $5.4 million. Sawyer's upper estimate makes the implicit assumption that the elasticity of substitution is directly related to the EC import demand elasticity which is unrealistic. It thus appears that Pomfret's estimates provide a better approximation to the size of the US manufacturing exports expected to be displaced by competing products from the three new members. About one-third of this export loss is concentrated in ten manufacturing products comprising parts, peripheral memory units and peripheral input/output units for automatic data processing machines, spark ignition engines, aircraft parts, parts for spark ignition engines, tinplate, cotton trousers, lubricating oils and mechanical shovels and excavators. The vast majority of the trade diversion effects against US exports of manufactures to the EC-9 is due to the accession of Spain.

However, US exports of manufactures will experience favourable external trade creation effects. US manufacturing exports to the three new members amounted to $8,455.1 million in 1980 - of which, three quarters were directed to Spain (table 7.2). On the basis of a rough estimate that the average tariff on manufacturing imports will fall in the three new members by about 50% to come down to the level of the CET and taking values for the export supply elasticity and import demand elasticity similar to those used by Pomfret (1985) we arrive at an estimated value of the size of the external trade creation in the markets of the three new members in favour of US manufacturing exports of around $247 million at 1979 prices (table 7.1). On balance, US exports of manufactures to the EC are expected to gain as a result of the enlargement. However, there is another effect of the second enlargement that will adversely affect some sensitive US manufacturing industries. As Hamilton (1986) has shown the accession of Greece, Portugal and Spain will give rise to indirect trade deflection involving the channelling of European, i.e. EC-9, supplies into exports to the US. This will result from the removal of the various NTBs (like VERs) that the EC-9 and EFTA maintained on Iberian (and Greek, before 1981) exports of textile and clothing products before accession and the fact that trade in manufactures between the EC and US is free of NTBs (with the exception of steel). Thus as the EC and EFTA will lift in 1990 their VERS and surveillance measures on textile and clothing imports from Spain and Portugal, prices in the EC-10 markets will be forced downwards. This will push European suppliers to divert part of their supplies to the US where their exports are not faced with any NTBs.

117

Portuguese wage rates in the clothing and textile industries are well below EC levels giving a clear competitive edge to Portuguese exports of these products to Community markets. This competitive strength will exert a downwards pressure on European prices and will induce established EC producers to redirect their trade to the US. This indirect trade deflection will be another consequence of the EC enlargement on the US manufacturing industries and will increase the adjustment pressures already faced by the US textile and clothing industries. The possibility of this type of indirect trade deflection will reduce the net gain to the US manufacturing (given in table 7.1) but it is expected that the balance will still be positive.

The net effects on American exports of agricultural products to the two Iberian economies are expected to be in the opposite direction. The extension of the CAP to the two economies will raise trade barriers on the average leading to trade destruction. The USA, as seen from table 7.2, has been an important supplier of agricultural products during the pre-accession period. For the two year period 1979-80, the US supplied 28 per cent of the total agricultural imports of Spain, 47 per cent of the total agricultural imports of Portugal and 13 per cent of the total agricultural imports of Greece. The import markets for cereals in particular maize were almost completely dominated by American suppliers in all three economies. As variable import levies are used to regulate external imports in these products the adverse effects against US exports are expected to be substantial. Moreover, the treaties of accession, particularly that of Portugal, introduce additional trade measures to regulate imports of cereals and oilseeds during the transition period.

The agricultural conflicts with the US of the Iberian enlargement can be summarised as follows:
(a)   The change in the Spanish system of an ad valorem duty of 20 per cent on cereals to the variable levy system of the CAP affects American exports to Spain of over $600 million. The US Department of Agriculture estimated that the change in the import system from ad valorem duties to variable levies will reduce American exports of cereals by $430 million. However Spanish cereal imports from the US have been falling regularly from 1980. From an average of 3.4 million tonnes during 1981/83 they fell to 2.3 million tonnes in 1984, rising again to 3.6 million tonnes in 1985 in anticipation of the introduction of the import levy system in March 1986.
(b)   The Portuguese treaty of accession stipulates that 15.5 per cent of Portugal's import needs of cereals will be reserved for EC suppliers. US exports covered around 90% of Portugal's import needs in cereals. The US is expected to lose exports of $90 million. The reservation of 15 per cent of the Portuguese markets for EC

118

supplies is explained by the fact that Portuguese imports of cereals are made through a state trading company thus making it difficult to ensure market regulated solutions. This arrangement of reserving 15 per cent of the market is expected to be temporary until Portugal introduces the market organisation envisaged by the CAP.

(c)   A quota on Portuguese imports from extra-EC suppliers of oilseeds is expected to add a loss of $60 million of American agricultural trade. American exports of oilseeds to Portugal averaged $195 million during the period 1983-85.

(d)   Outside agriculture, disputes may also emerge in the fisheries sector. Spain and Portugal, both fishing nations of considerable importance, have been linked with the United States through separate "governing international Fishery Agreements" (GIFA) entitling them to fish in the economic zone of the United States. Both Spain and Portugal must eventually (i.e. at the time of the expiry of their GIFA with the USA or, at the latest, after a further year) be integrated within the EC fisheries treaty with the US. This accession of the two Iberian countries to the EC's GIFA with the US may force a re-examination of the EC-US fisheries treaty. The two new members have fishing quotas that they would like to maintain e.g. by adding them to the quotas allocated to the EC-10. It is obvious that US agreement is required. Such agreement may be given in exchange for concessions in other areas of trade. This is why the fisheries issue may become another source of potential conflict.

(e)   The Commission of the EC argued, with reason, that the change in the import regime of the Iberian countries could also bring gains to US agricultural exports. The rise of the domestic Spanish price of cereals as a result of the application of the CAP rules will encourage the use of cheaper substitutes in the livestock production sector of the country. A large part of the expected increase in the imports of cereals substitutes (e.g. corngluten feed, soya beans) will be supplied by the US. These substitutes will be imported in Spain and Portugal from 1991 onwards at a zero customs duty. The US Administration regards this as an uncertain gain because of the prospects of renegotiating tariff rates on these products in the framework of the forthcoming GATT discussions on international trade in agricultural products.

4 Response to threats in market shares

How does a country whose exports are threatened by trade policy initiatives of other countries respond to safeguard its interests? Caves and Jones (1973) building upon Johnson's (1954) earlier work suggest two alternatives: bribe or retaliation. Bribing the offending country (in this case the EC) to remove its trade barriers is not a realistic option for the US since it would have meant asking the EC to

119

dismantle its agricultural policy. Retaliation appears as the only other option left. This is not however an entirely accurate description of the set of choices available. For within the present system of international trade, disputes from the formation (or extension) of customs unions can be resolved within the procedures of article 24 of the GATT treaty.

However, this time the US Administration has decided to reject the GATT road to trade conflict resolution. The GATT disputes settlement procedure proved to be fairly lengthy as shown by the time taken to reach a panel decision on the US complaint on EC preferences to Mediterranean citrus fruit producers. This time the US was concerned with a quick resolution of the trade dispute as it was burdened by a serious crisis in its domestic agricultural sector and exposed to a serious trade balance deficit. Secondly, the US Administration has become frustrated by its lack of success to persuade the GATT council to endorse the panels' recommendations. The EC with its network of preferential trading agreements has now created within GATT a web of mutual involvement that creates an appropriate climate of blocking such an endorsement. Indicative of this frustration is the description of the GATT as a "paper mouse" by US legislators (Smith, 1983).

Thirdly, as the dispute centred on agricultural trade, the US Administration was fully aware of the elusive nature of the GATT provisions on primary products. As a nation that benefits from the formal waivers allowing countries to maintain legislation contrary to the GATT in the agricultural sector, the US realised that it could not master the credibility necessary to complain successfully about non-observance by others of the GATT rules (Wellenstein, 1986).

Thus when the first part of the second enlargement of the EC was completed with the accession of Greece, the US Administration declined to take part in GATT negotiations for possible compensation under article 24 when invited by the Commission of the EC because it was not prepared to counterbalance losses in agricultural exports with gains in manufacturing exports to the Greek market. This type of response was also to be followed when the Iberian enlargement was concluded. The Commission of the EC invited the USA to negotiate within the GATT framework but on the condition that a global approach will be adopted taking simultaneously into account both agricultural and manufacturing trade and considering compensation for the net balance. The US was not happy about this approach and consequently invoked at an early stage the threat of retaliation. The US position on GATT compensation negotiation procedures has also shifted from previous practices. The American government's refusal to follow past GATT practices was explained on the grounds that the

US should have been consulted **before** the actual conclusion of the treaties of accession of the Iberian countries. Although this may be based on a narrow interpretation of article 24, it is unrealistic to expect the EC to give the US a delaying power over plans to enlarge itself.

Early in 1986, the US Administration published a list of products to be subjected to retaliatory action for the loss of markets in the Iberian region as a result of the extension of the CAP to the two new members. The retaliatory action was targeted to the specific sources of market loss for the US exporters. To retaliate against the introduction of a quota of 15 per cent of cereals imports into Portugal reserved for EC-10 the US proposed restrictive measures against imports of biscuits and sweets, confectionary products (chocolates), fruit juices and fresh apples. In retaliation to restrictions on US sales of oilseeds to Portugal, restrictive measures were proposed against imports of white wine of EC origin. American sanctions on cheeses, pork and beef products, olives (preserved), a few other food products and leather were proposed to retaliate against market losses of cereals exports to Spain. The first US announcement in April 1986 set no specific timetable. Later a deadline was set for 31 December 1986 which was subsequently extended to 31 January 1987.

The type of retaliation envisaged was a 200 per cent duty on EC exports to the US of the above foods and beverages scheduled to become effective on 31 January 1987 unless a satisfactory solution to the US access to the Iberian agricultural import markets was found. The Commission of the EC responded almost immediately to the first retaliatory moves of the US by publishing its own hit list of US products against whom counter-retaliation measures were to be introduced. The Brussels lists included sunflower seeds, honey, animal fats, plums, horsemeat, fruit juices, fresh foliage, pop-corn, ambergris, soya cakes, corngluten feed, almonds, wheat and rice.

The US Administration timed its decision to coincide with the introduction of the CAP for cereals in Spain which started on 1 March 1986. Unlike previous trade disputes with the EC which usually originated in Congress, this time the move for retaliation was a White House initiative - a factor that served to underline the changing American mood on the trade conflicts with the EC.

The counter-reprisals proposed by the Commission of the EC failed to exert a decisive impact in speeding up the resolution of the conflict because they were not unequivocally backed by the Council of Ministers. If a tit-for-tat approach is to produce a quick resolution then it must have credibility. When the Council of Ministers met in Luxembourg on 21 April 1986 - a little while after the US move for retaliation - it failed to fully back the Commission proposals for counteraction. Only the French and the Portuguese governments showed unreserved enthusiasm for the move proposed by the Commission. The Federal Republic, the Netherlands and Denmark showed remarkable reticence. This probably led to the prolongation of the trade dispute which at times looked like degenerating into an open trade war. If the so-called new Community trade instrument can be used without the prior approval of the Council of Ministers, it may help to resolve trade conflicts more speedily.

As it happened, the dispute lasted for about 10 months and was settled on 29 January 1987 after intense talks covering all-night sessions and satellite communications between Brussels and Washington. The agreement reached conceded (a) Community allowances for non-EC exporters to sell up to 2 million tonnes of maize yearly into the Spanish market and up to 300,000 tonnes of sorghum into the Portuguese market, at reduced tariffs. This compromise is far below the 4 million tonnes of cereals to the two markets with 2.8 million tonnes reserved for US suppliers demanded originally by the US negotiator Clayton Yeutter. The US target of 4 million tonnes was unrealistic as it is above the level of the estimated Spanish feedgrain import needs of 3.2 million tonnes per annum. But it is also above the original EC offer of 1.6 tonnes for both cereals and sorghum. (b) an abandonment of the right of the EC-10 under the Portuguese accession treaty to reserve 15 per cent of Portugal's cereals markets for EC suppliers. The US National Corn Growers Association has already expressed concern about this agreement because of its lack of enforcement provisions (The Times, 31 January 1987).

5 Retaliation as a Strategic Trade Policy Option

The 1986 trade conflict with the US over the extension of the European customs union raises two interesting questions. The first relates to the economic determinants of retaliation, i.e. to the factors that determine the use of retaliation as the appropriate response to other governments' trade policies. The second question is the extent to which retaliation is the best option for a government to use and in particular for the US to adopt in its handling of the trade disputes generated from the application of the CAP to the Iberian economies. The first question is a matter of positive political economy, the second of normative analysis.

The trade conflict from the Iberian enlargement demonstrated a shift in the policy of the US towards both the use of the GATT system and the handling of its disputes with the EC. The US Administration was not prepared to follow the slow process of the GATT panel investigations and recommendations mindful of the fate of previous recommendations in the GATT council meetings. The reluctance of the US government to follow past practice and negotiate within GATT for compensation taking into account simultaneously both agricultural and manufacturing trade benefits from external trade creation and losses from trade diversion and trade destruction, reflects basic changes in US attitudes towards strategies for trade liberalisation.

As other cases have shown, US preferences are now in favour of selective trade liberalisation, i.e. liberalisation focusing on specific protectionist measures or granted selectively to some countries (Weintraub, 1985). This shift from the GATT-based approach to a selective trade liberalisation approach is partly a reaction to the proliferation of preferential trading arrangements. Selective protection is to be tackled by initiatives that are similarly selective so that pockets of protective measures are removed by action targeted against them rather than through concessions in other sectors.

Another change in the US policy is that this time the American government insisted that the GATT procedures required negotiations with injured parties before the actual extension of a customs union. Although such a procedure had not been followed in the past, it appears that the interpretation requiring prior (rather than after the event) negotiations is more within the spirit of article 24 of the GATT. In addition the US invoked the threat of retaliation at a fairly early stage in the emergence of the trade dispute in variance with past conflicts (e.g. the Mediterranean citrus fruit case) where such action was contemplated at a later stage thus indicating the preference of the American government for a more coercive form of action in place of adjudication. In order to explain the use of retaliation as a strategic trade policy option, it will be helpful to employ the basic framework of the models of political choice that emphasise the role of interest groups and stress the benefits and costs of interest group organisation. Retaliation measures are normally sector specific and are thus likely to reflect the motivation and the organisational efforts of the corresponding interest groups (Caves, 1976).

In a modern democratic state the use of trade retaliation measures will be determined by the interplay of several factors that encourage the demand for such measures by key socioeconomic groups and various factors that explain the gains expected by those legally entitled to supply such measures. One can envisage the existence of a politico-economic market for retaliation where the intensity and the extent of the retaliatory action taken by one government against another's trade policies are determined by the interaction of the demand for and the supply of retaliation. The demand for retaliation is determined by

123

factors that parallel the demand for protection (Hughes, 1986). The determinants of demand for retaliation can be categorised into two groups: macroeconomic and industry specific.

A number of **macroeconomic** determinants of the demand for retaliation can be identified:

The maintenance of an overvalued currency and the presence of a sizeable and accelerating trade deficit often lead to demands for retaliation. In such circumstances many groups of exporters find it difficult to compete in foreign markets. Indeed, most of the trade conflicts with the EC have coincided with periods of overvaluation of the dollar or worrying American trade deficits. Concern for the effects of the CAP on American exports of agricultural trade was raised for the first time by the end of the decade of the 1960s when a high fixed dollar exchange rate was one of the principal reasons for the stagnation of these exports. And it is significant that the US Administration resorted to the threat of retaliation in 1986 two years after the trade balance of the United States with the EC turned from a persistently surplus position since 1958 into a deficit of ECU 8,000 million in 1984 and ECU 15,000 million in 1985.

The more crucial the role of exports is for the national economy the more pressures will be generated for retaliatory action when exporters are faced with market restricting measures of competing nations. Over the past 15 years the US economy has progressively become more sensitive to global trade conditions. During this period one has witnessed the progressive domestication of the US trade policy, i.e domestic prosperity has become more sensitive to trade policy. Moreover, in an economy increasingly sensitive to world trade conditions and with a high fixed dollar exchange rate, trade policy will tend to adopt a strategic posture and move towards a non-cooperative activism.

The lower the degree of the multinationalisation of production the stronger will be the lobbying activities for retaliation. Industries with a low degree of multinationalisation will tend to have limited options to substitute exports for international production. This explains why so many of the retaliation threats are for safeguarding the interests of agricultural producers.

The more extensively foreign competitors subsidise their exports the stronger will be the demand of the domestic producers for retaliation.

Finally, lobbying for retaliation will tend to increase if the domestic factor prices in the export sector rise above their productivity as in this case the competitiveness of exportables will be reduced.

Industry-specific determinants of retaliation include such characteristics as the size of the industry, its degree of size and geographical concentration, its level of organisation and its ratio of exports to total sales. The larger the industry the more significant are likely to be economies of scale in lobbying efforts for retaliation. The more geographically concentrated the industry is the easier it will be for it to recruit the necessary allies in putting up pressure for retaliatory action. The higher the size concentration of the industry the more limited are any 'free rider' problems to lobbying activities. Support for such activities leading to retaliation will be easier to marshall with a well organised industry. If the ratio of exports to total sales is high then the industry's urge for action to objectionable policies of other nations will tend to be strong. The link between lobbying for retaliation and industry characteristics provides an answer to the puzzle of former EC Commissioner R. Dahrendorf who remarked in the 1960s that "the California and Arizona Citrus' Growers Association sometimes seemed to be directing the whole thrust of American trade policy" (quoted in Wallace, 1982).

The cost of supply of retaliation depends on national political structures and institutions as well as on the effectiveness of the rules and procedures of the international trading system. The existence of an effective system of international rules in settling trade disputes acts as a factor that makes the supply of retaliation costlier. The vacuum of consistent and binding rules on international trade in agricultural products partly explains the high incidence of trade conflicts in agricultural trade. It is not only a set of rules that is required. To ensure that the rules are obeyed some international body of a judicial character is essential. Here too the GATT framework leaves much to be desired. By reducing the degree of national discretion in the application of international rules, one helps to decrease the transaction costs of *ad hoc* bilateral bargaining. The cost of supply of retaliation becomes lower when the political gains of tolerating injurious trade policy actions of other nations are limited and of decreasing significance. When the political gains from European integration were perceived to be high by the US governments, their attitudes to the CAP and the preferential trading practices of the EC were less hostile. Dilution of the political contribution of European integration to the Alliance made the US eventually lukewarm towards the further enlargement of the EC.

6 Concluding Remarks

The above analysis of the determinants of demand and supply of retaliation suggests a number of ways of minimising the sources of trade conflicts and the potential dangers of leapfrogging protectionism and destructive trade wars.

Reducing the demand for retaliation is one route; raising the cost of supply of retaliation is another. One way of reducing the demand for retaliation is to eliminate market distortions and adopt appropriate macroeconomic policies for the purpose of maintaining realistic exchange rates. Another important factor leading to a reduction in the demand for retaliation is the elimination of export refunds and the sources creating the need for the use of these subsidies. In the context of the US-EC trade relations this essentially means reform of the CAP by bringing European support prices closer to the world prices. Such an alternative seems rather remote as the Community's Green Paper on Agriculture (Commission of the EC, 1985b) makes it clear. This leaves as the most likely alternative for eliminating some of the sources of international trade conflicts the reform of the international trading system.

The disputes settlement procedure of the GATT have proved to be cumbersome and ineffective leading to the frustration of injured parties and the emergence of trade conflicts. Article 24 of the GATT rules needs streamlining to eliminate the possibility of the establishment or extension of customs unions that set external tariffs exceeding the average tariff of the partners. Finally, the integration of agricultural trade into the main body of the GATT through the removal of 'waivers' will go a long way towards eliminating a major source of trade conflicts. The forthcoming Uruguay round of MTNs has raised hopes that a system of rules designed towards the liberalisation of world agricultural trade may be eventually devised. The Commission of the EC (Green Europe, 1986) has marginally shifted its position in this matter by asking for more refined rules for international agricultural trade to reduce the unjustified costs of cut-throat competition. But for its concessions, it demands reciprocal sacrifices from its trading partners. However, what the Commission regards as new refined rules for international agricultural trade is in effect a rearrangement of the structure of agricultural protection. Such, a rearrangement will involve the reduction of protection in some products that goes hand in hand with stronger protection for others without increasing the general level of protection of European agriculture. A more balanced framework of external protection may reduce the trade injuries to the US but at the same time it will have a different impact on the various types of agricultural production within the EC. In the last analysis, the credibility of the EC regarding its commitment to liberalise world trade in agricultural products depends on its ability to tackle successfully its internal market problems. For what is needed for a less friction-ridden world is a reduction in the average level of protection of European agriculture and not a mere streamlining of the present structure.

The prospects for a comprehensive review of the GATT rules that will strengthen the use of international adjudication in disciplining countries in the use of export subsidies and other means of unfair competition in agricultural trade are thus not very promising. For they require additionally considerable changes of the US farm policy. From the very beginning of the GATT the US insisted in obtaining a waiver from GATT rules in order to protect its cotton, dairy and sugar industries with quantitative import restrictions.

In 1985 attempts were made by the US to introduce a new law limiting EC wine exports to the US. The EC and ten other GATT members launched a complaint against the US. In general, GATT rules as they exist are relatively effective in deterring new restrictions rather than in removing existing ones operating under past waiver agreements.

The difficulties of a new GATT for agricultural trade suggest to US policy makers alternative approaches to cope with the challenge of the EC's CAP particularly in third markets. These alternatives include negotiations and *ad hoc* bilateral bargaining, collusion, retaliation and competition. Paarlberg (1986) has shown that none of the first three alternative options is a wise choice for the US. Bilateral bargaining apart from its high transaction costs (Corden, 1986) creates an environment that strengthens the lobbying activities of the agricultural interest groups thus leading to frustration in the emergence of a desired solution. Retaliation is bound at the end to lead to more substantial losses for countries which have much larger agricultural exports to protect. If it disintegrates into an open trade war, it will thus inflict higher losses on the US. A collusion based on an agreement with the EC 'not to compete' in third country markets is not only difficult to conclude but even more difficult to monitor. Given the decision making structures within the EC it is doubtful whether the latter has the capacity to honour a market-fixing arrangement. Competition as the best available US policy response to the CAP and an appropriate US agricultural trade strategy is difficult to pursue in an economic environment characterised by large macroeconomic imbalances and high exchange rates. Restoring domestic fiscal discipline in the US is a prerequisite for the use of the competition alternative as a credible US strategy for responding to the CAP.

Table 7.1: Effects of the Formation and Enlargements of the European Community on US Trade

	Gains	Losses	Net Balance
	(in millions of US dollars)		
1. Formation of EC-6			
External trade creation in manufactures	9,000[a]	-	-
Trade diversion against manufacturing exports	-	2,000[a]	-
Net trade diversion and/or destruction) in agricultural exports	-	1,300[a]	-
Net trade effect			+5,700[a]
2. First Enlargement (EC-9)			
External trade creation in manufactures	5,300[a]	-	-
Trade diversion against manufacturing exports	-	3,900[a]	-
Net trade diversion (and/or destruction) against agricultural exports	-	1,400[a]	-
Net trade effect			0
3. Second Enlargement (EC-12)			
External trade creation in manufactures	247.0[b]	-	-
Trade diversion against manufacturing exports	-	1.4[b]	-
Net trade diversion and/or trade destruction) affecting agricultural exports to Spain and Portugal	-	580.0[b]	-
Net trade effect			-334.4[b]

(a) valued at 1969/70 prices; (b) valued at 1979 prices

Sources: For (1) and (2): M.E.Kreinin (1974)
For (3) : own estimates for external trade creation, estimates by R. Pomfret (1985) for trade diversion in manufactures and estimates by the US Department of Agriculture for trade diversion against agricultural imports.

Table 7.2: Imports of the Three New Members from the United States

average 1979-80

Product Groups	SPAIN US$ (million)	SPAIN p.c. of total	PORTUGAL US$ (million)	PORTUGAL p.c. of total	GREECE US $ (million)	GREECE p.c. of total
Manufactures (S.I.T.C. 5, 6, 7 & 8)	1,660.4	13.8	224.6	6.8	240.6	3.8
Agricultural Products (S.I.T.C. 0, 1 & 4)	885.6	28.1	479.1	46.7	117.9	13.2
of which: maize (044)	519.3	83.6	330.2	99.8	97.5	96.8
other cereals	109.2	55.0	113.3	56.5	0.3	1.0
All Products	3,772.0	12.7	889.9	11.3	475.5	4.7

Source: OECD, Trade by Commodities, Series C.

CHAPTER EIGHT

The External Trade Effects of the EC's Integrated Mediterranean Programmes

1 Introduction

After a long gestation period commencing from the time of the Commission's report pursuant to the Mandate of 30 May 1980, the EC Council has formally adopted the regulations implementing the Integrated Mediterranean Programmes (IMPs) in July 1985 bringing them into force as from 1 August 1985. The IMPs have been conceived as an adjustment assistance policy to enable the Mediterranean regions of the European Community of Ten to face successfully the competitive challenge of the Iberian enlargement of the Community. In addition, the Commission in its original proposals (Commission of the EC, 1983) regarded the programmes as providing assistance for the rehabilitation of those regions and sectors that have been put at a disadvantage as a result of increased import competition from the associated Mediterranean countries. In the words of the Commission "enlargement to include Portugal and Spain **and** the development of preferential relations in the Mediterranean area are accentuating the problems (of marketing their traditional produce) by requiring adjustment efforts of these regions and imposing constraints on their development decisions" (because of the lack of) "necessary resources to consolidate efforts to switch to new crops and products" (p.4). The programmes thus aim at facilitating structural adaptation to trade-induced change. The need for a positive adjustment policy as opposed to market coordination adjustment is justified by the structural deficiencies of these regions (microeconomic inflexibilities, nature of their products and their conditions of access to the market etc.).

However, the IMPs are qualitatively different from the more traditional form of adjustment policies discussed in the literature. Their aim is not just to pave the way for **general** import liberalisation but for a **limited** liberalisation involving the opening up of the markets of the established members of a customs union to the competitive pressures of the new members. Apart from the general danger of degeneration into protective devices, adjustment policies of the type envisaged by the IMPs run the additional danger of reorienting the production structure towards a non-optimal division of labour from the world viewpoint in the sense that resource reallocation is conditioned not by world relative prices but by distorted price signals influenced by the various trade impediments that characterise the EC's common external commercial policy. Thus although the adjustment measures involved in the IMPs have been designed to accommodate competitive changes primarily within the internal market of the enlarged EC, nevertheless they are likely to have implications for third country producers and the external trade of the EC.

The objective of this chapter is to examine the trade implications of the adjustment policies contemplated within the IMPs and in particular their effects on the export prospects on the non-member Mediterranean countries. Before attempting this exercise the chapter looks first at the nature and the size of the adjustment problems faced by the Mediterranean regions of the EC-Ten following the Iberian enlargment of the Community (section 2). In section 3 the chapter examines the adjustment measures of the IMPs. Section 4 evaluates the efficiency implications of these measures in the light of conventional analysis of positive adjustment policies. Building upon the findings of sections 3 and 4, the chapter then focuses on its primary objective i.e. the implications of the IMPs on the external trade relations of the EC. It specifies the links between the measures adopted by the IMPs and the trade interests of third countries and comes to some tentative conclusions regarding the type of trade and the groups of countries likely to be affected.

2 Nature and Size of the Adjustment Problems

The intensity of the adjustment problems generated by the second enlargement depends on the level of the pre-enlargement barriers to trade between the EC-10 and the two Iberian economies, the similarity in the production and export structures of the Mediteranean members of the EC-10 and the two new members, the supply response and potential of the Iberian producers and the capacity for adjustment of the EC-10 regions directly competing with the new members.

Studies of the similarity of production and export structures in relation to predicted changes in trade barriers and relative prices have produced a number of lists of 'vulnerable' products and industries to the competitive thrust from the Iberian enlargement (Commission of the EC, 1981a, 1981b, 1984f). The consensus emerging from these studies is that the Iberian enlargement poses adjustment problems chiefly to the agricultural sector of the Mediterranean regions of EC-10 but has moderate and to some extent balanced consequences for the industrial sectors of these regions.

Two alternative approaches have been followed to identify 'vulnerable' agricultural production in the Mediterranean regions of EC-10. Alessandrini, Fotia and Vinci (Commission of the EC, 1981b) compile their list of 'vulnerable' exports by classifying products according to whether the Mediterranean countries of the EC-10 and the Iberian countries specialise or not in certain production.

Countries of regions that are net exporters of the product are classified as being specialised in its production. Net imports signify a lack of specialisation. 'Vulnerable' production in the Mediterranean regions of EC-10 was identified with products where both these regions and the Iberian economies specialise. These researchers have found that about one third (32.61 per cent) of the value of Italian agricultural production falls in this group of sensitive products. To this group they added another type of sensitive production, namely products in which the Mediterranean regions of the EC-10 are net importers (no specialisation) but the Iberian countries are net exporters (have a high degree of specialisation). This brought the proportion of the value of Italian agricultural output vulnerable to competition from the Iberian peninsula to approximately 37.5 per cent (1976-77 production years). According to the analysis of these researchers products with a high intensity of adjustment problems include olive oil, table wines and industrial tomatoes. A more comprehensive analysis linking demand-supply balances at the Community level and differences between the CAP support prices and local prices in the Iberian economies before enlargement was reported in another Commisson study (Commission of the EC, 1984f).

On the basis of the different combinations of the above two market features (demand-supply balances and price ratios) a sensitivity indicator was assigned to each product by convention ranging from a positive value for products in which enlargement could have a favourable impact on the market situation to a negative value in the opposite case. The classification of products according to their market features and the sensitivity indicator assigned to each product group appear in Table 1. Regions with serious adjustment problems are then identified on the basis of their agricultural production structures. The sensitivity indicator for each product appearing in Table 8.1 is weighted by the proportional share of this product in overall regional agricultural production. Summing up the weighted sensitivity indicators over all products, a global index of vulnerability is derived that enables us to identify the regions with the more acute adjustment problems - these being the regions with a high global vulnerability index.

On the basis of the analysis underlying the construction of table 8.1 regions with serious adjustment problems in their agricultural sector will be those with a high concentration of agricultural production in products where simultaneously
(a)   there is a surplus situation in the Community of 12
(b)   the prices in the new members at the commencement of their transition period were below Community prices and

Table 8.1: Classification of Agricultural Products according to their sensitivity to enlargement

Market Features:		Products	Sensitivity Indicator
Demand-Supply Balance*	Ratio of Iberian to EC-10 prices*		
		Vulnerable Products (I)	
		Olive Oil	-10.0
MS	ML	Wine	- 8.0
		Fresh and Processed Tomatoes	- 7.5
		Lemons	- 7.5
		Vulnerable Products (II)	
		Table grapes	- 6.0
S	L	Peaches	- 6.0
		Cauliflower	- 6.0
		New potatoes	- 5.0
		Vulnerable Products (III)	
RS	L	Other fruit (except apples)	- 3.0
		Other vegetables	- 3.0
		Neutral Products	
E/D	RL	Vegetable oils, rice, tobacco, lamb	- 0.0
		Eggs, poultry, durum wheat	- 0.0
		Assisted Products	
E/D	H	Cereals	+ 2.0
E/D	L	Sugar	+ 0.7
E	H	Milk	+ 0.4
E	H	Beef, veal, pigmeat	+ 0.2

* MS = Considerable Excess Supply   ** ML = considerably below one
  S = Excess Supply   L   = lower than one
 RS = Low Excess Supply   RL = close to one but still
  B = Market in Balance   below one
E/D = EC-10 Net Exporter   H   = more than one
       or EC-12 Net Importer
  E = Limited exports by EC-10

Source : Commission of the EC (1984)

(c)   the elasticity of supply with respect to price is high in the Iberian countries.

Industrial adjustment problems appear to be rather limited if one judges their intensity from the similarity of the export structures of the Iberian countries and the Community of Ten (table 8.2). Community exports are competing directly only to a limited extent with Portuguese exports but far more extensively with Spanish exports. However, the coefficients of trade overlap are much higher than those for the EC as a whole when Italian export structures are compared with the export structures of the two Iberian countries. Portuguese and Greek export structures show a much higher similarity than Portuguese and Community export structures. Spanish and Greek export structures appear to overlap far less than Spanish and Community export structures.

Table 8.2: Coefficients of Trade Overlap : Manufacturing Export Structures (1976-77)

	Portugal	Spain
EC-9	0.373	0.737
Italy	0.501	0.785
Greece	0.628	0.516

Source : Commission of the EC, The Effects of the Enlargement of the EC on the Italian Regions, Internal Documentation on Community Regional Policy, No. 13, October 1981.

A comparison of export and import shares (table 8.3) shows that Italy and France have far more intensive trade in industrial goods with Portugal and Spain than the rest of the Community.

Imports from the Iberian countries accounted in 1980 for 4.4% and 3.0 per cent of French and Italian imports respectively as against 2.5 per cent for the EC as a whole. French and Italian exports to the Iberian countries represented in 1980 3.7 per cent and 5.4 per cent of their total exports respectively as against 2.8 per cent for the EC as a whole. However, adjustment problems can be identified more concretely only by following a product by product analysis of the evolution of the indexes of revealed comparative advantages in the Iberian countries and the countries of the Community of Ten. Improvements over time in the index of revealed comparative advantage indicate how successfully the countries concerned were in raising their ability to export particular products. Changes over time in the revealed comparative advantage indexes of the two Iberian countries (Donges and Schatz, 1985) indicate that the two countries enjoy comparative advantages in manufactured products with a high input of unskilled labour (clothing, footwear and similar) or with a low technological content and limited processing operations (textiles, ceramics, leather and leather products, wood products, iron and steel, metal products and similar). EC trade in clothing, textiles and motor vehicles with the Iberian countries is characterised by large deficits ($527 million, $330 million and $520 million respectively in 1980).

The Community countries and regions that are characterised by a high concentration of production in sectors where the Iberian countries have high and rising values of revealed comparative advantage indexes will be those likely to experience intense adjustment problems. Regions and countries with a more balanced industrial structure (i.e. with a structure characterised by the presence of sectors likely to expand their exports to the Iberian countries because of the weak revealed comparative advantage of the latter) will be able to adjust relatively smoothly. Regions with limited alternative employment opportunities and substantial factor and product market rigidities will experience serious difficulties in adjusting to the competitive pressures of the enlargement. The findings of the Italian study (Commission of the EC, 1981b) indicate that whilst for the country as a whole there are sufficient opportunities for counterbalancing the negative effects from the stiffer competition in products intensive in low skills manpower and involving limited processing operations with advantages from sectors to be favoured by the enlargement of the market, nevertheless the locations of the two groups of industries (i.e. those experiencing negative and those expecting positive effects) often differ. Given market factor immobilities and other market rigidities this development leaves some regions with more adjustment problems to be solved. Vulnerable industrial sectors are defined as those where the Iberian countries have had high and rising values in their indexes of comparative advantages. Assisted or favoured sectors are those where the Iberian countries have low and/or declining values of their indexes of revealed comparative advantage. Regions with serious industrial adjustment problems stimulated from the stiffer competition of the EC enlargement will be those with a high concentration of vulnerable sectors and a low degree of concentration of favoured sectors. Such regions with industrial adjustment problems arising from the second enlargement of the EC are the Mezzogiorno in Italy, the regions of Aquitaine, Midi Pyrénées, Languedoc-Roussillon and Corsica in France and all Greek regions.

However, Delfaud's research (Commission of the EC, 1981a) showed that certain departments (arrondissements) within the first two French regions were expected to experience net favourable effects, making thus the adjustment problems more manageable because the required factor mobility would be limited. Excluding the departments just mentioned, the rest of these four French regions are characterised by a

135

heavy concentration of traditional sectors like textiles, clothing, leather and footwear, and wood products - precisely the sectors where Spanish revealed comparative advantage appears strong. And contrary to what is generally observed in EC-Spanish trade, these French regions import from Spain increasingly processed goods whilst they export unprocessed or little processed products to Spain.

Table 8.3: **Share of EC's manufacturing trade accounted by the Iberian countries, 1980**

	Imports	Exports
Belgium/Luxembourg	1.2	1.4
Germany	2.2	2.3
Denmark	1.5	1.4
France	4.4	3.7
United Kingdom	2.3	2.1
Italy	3.0	5.4
Ireland	1.2	2.0
Holland	1.2	2.0
EC-9	2.5	2.8
Greece	0.3	1.8

Source : Commission of the EC, the Regions of Europe, COM(84) Final/2, 1984.

Greece faces industrial adjustment problems from the Iberian enlargement of the Community not dissimilar to those of the Mezzogiorno. With Greek industrial exports heavily concentrated (about 55%) in textiles and clothing, competition from the new members will give rise to some pressing adjustment issues.

Having reviewed the sources and indicated the expected intensity of the adjustment problems in the agricultural and industrial sectors of the Mediterranean regions of the EC-10, we now proceed to summarise briefly in section 3 the basic features of the IMPs and to enquire in section 4 how far they fulfil the key requirements of an adjustment policy programme.

3 The basic features of the IMPs

The IMPs are designed to implement in a coordinated way over a limited period of 7 years Community actions to facilitate the adjustment of the southern regions of the EC-10 to the new competitive environment created by the Iberian enlargement. The actions which can be financed by the IMPs fall into the following five categories: investment expenditure in **physical infrastructure**, expenditure for the development and better use of **human** resources, **rationalisation** investment aimed to improve quality of the product if necessary by changing to different varieties, investment expenditure for **restructuring** and **conversion** to switch to new product lines that do not aggravate the market situation in the Community and expenditure for the **relocation** (transfer) of production or the **cessation** of production in agricultural areas. It must be noted that measures for conversion to other lines of production are backed up by initiatives aimed at guaranteeing a satisfactory income to the farmers. The various actions are expected to support each other and be highly interlinked. This is what makes these programmes integrated. For example conversion to alternative crops is expected to be coordinated with actions on physical infrastructure and better use of human resources like irrigation, reparcelling of land, creation of producer groups, back up and advisory services. Actions under the IMPs are either **general** or **selective**. General measures are those that are not targeted to specific products or industries like physical improvement measures in agricultural regions (reparcelling, land improvement), support measures for small and medium sized enterprises in the non-agricultural sector, infrastructure to improve the viability of rural areas or for the development of job creating activities, training and labour market back-up measures. Selective measures are targeted to specific products or industries by taking into account the potential of each area and the particular characteristics of its predominant forms of production. Selective measures are thus more interventionist and raise interesting questions regarding the ability of governments and international organisations to pick up winners in a dynamic market environment. Important in this respect is the institutional approach adopted in implementing the measures i.e. whether structural adjustment assistance is managed by public administration bodies or market oriented banking institutions.

From the point of view of the sectoral distribution of the expenditure for the IMPs, two kinds of measures can be distinguished: (a) measures for the agricultural sector aimed to improve production, marketing and processing structures and to bring agricultural production more into line with market requirements (b) measures to create alternative non-agricultural employment by developing other activities in rural areas (e.g. rural tourism) and to provide the facilities needed to repair certain weaknesses in the regional socioeconomic fabric.

In terms of the sectoral allocation of the total expenditure of the IMPs (6,600 million ECU) agriculture is the most substantial recipient accounting for 50% (table 8.4).

Development of activities in the non-agricultural sector are expected to absorb about 21 per cent of total spending. Priorities within the non-agricultural sector include rural tourism, renewable sources of energy, craft industries and the strengthening of the financial, informational and technological basis of small and medium sized manufacturing and service firms. The remaining expenditure is earmarked for the provision of general infrastructure, training and research (17.6 per cent) and for the fisheries and forestry sectors (about 11 per cent).

Table 8.4: Sectoral Allocation of the Expenditure for the IMPs (percentages)

Agriculture (including advisory services)	50.0
Forestry	5.8
Fisheries	5.4
Non-Agricultural Development	21.2
General Infrastructure, Training and Research	17.6

Source : Commission of the EC, The Commission's Proposals for the Integrated Mediterranean Programmes, COM(83)24 final, Brussels, 1983.

The financial assistance for IMPs will consist of allocations of 4,100 million ECU from the Community budget and EIB loans totalling 2500 million ECU from own resources and from the resources of the New Community Instrument. Of the total allocations from the Community budget only 1,600 million ECU will represent additional spending; the rest (2500 million ECU) will come from the existing funds (ERDF, ESF, Guidance Section of EAGGF). The IMPs submitted by Greece will qualify for an amount of 2,000 million ECU from both categories of the budget. This leaves an average around 9 billion FF per annum for France and 150 billion lire for Italy (which spends only for its operations in the Mezzogiorno a sum of 10,000 billion lire per annum).

The level of the Community's participation in funding the various projects varies according to the type of operation with a special rate for Greece which may be as much as 70 per cent of costs. EC participation will be through investment subsidies or subsidies for training and research and development as well as in the form of income support or compensatory allowances to farmers. The level of investment subsidies varies and tends to be lower in projects expected to yield more immediate returns (as e.g. with investment by the agricultural processing industry or with the marketing of agricultural produce). Income support is earmarked for farmers in areas where a certain level of population must be maintained whilst compensatory allowances are planned at a high rate.

138

It should be stressed that some of the policy instruments proposed for the attainment of the objectives of the IMPs involve no new measures but rather a broadening of existing measures or extending their geographical scope (table 4). All in all the IMPs involve the combined use of 40 types of policy measures of which only about one third are adding new instruments to the Community's policies. A more detailed list of the type of instruments used for implementing IMPs appears in the appendix.

Table 8. 5: Analysis of the Measures Proposed for the IMPs by degree of innovativeness

		Number
1.	Entirely new	13
2.	Involving only extension of the geographical scope of existing measures	10
3.	Involving a mixture of geographical extension and broadening of existing measures	7
4.	Increasing the level of assistance (including covering of new products)	10
		—
	Total	40
		—

Source : Commission of the EC (1983).

We now look in some detail into the various measures of rationalisation and reconversion or restructuring of the Mediterranean regions covered by the IMPs. This is an important prerequisite in order to assess the implications of the IMPs on the trade interests of third countries. The rationalisation and reconversion measures for agriculture are clearly differentiated between inland and lowland subregions with the former encouraged towards the development of certain types of livestock production and the latter assisted to move primarily towards the cultivation of new varieties or entirely new crops for which the market situation within the EC is not going to be aggravated. Measures for cattle farming in lowland subregions and of integrating stock rearing in inland subregions with finishing enterprises in lowland subregions are also envisaged.

The financial subsidies and soft loans for the modernisation and restructuring of livestock farming involve (a) a series of initiatives to increase animal feeding stuff like renewing pasture and meadows and using them more intensively plus the development of protein and fodder crops (maize, sorghum etc. particularly in the coastal and lowland subregions of Italy) through the provision of selected seeds, water supplies and the spread of mechanisation methods on the basis of producers groups; (b) the extension of sheep and goat farming through measures like improving grazing, better infrastructure of sheep and goat farms, aids for milk testing, health protection and genetic improvement; (c) the support of cattle farming in lowland subregions by increasing the productivity of herds by means of genetic improvement schemes and aids for building and improving livestock housing. Extending livestock farming into horses is to be encouraged in Italy.

Measures to rationalise and restructure crop production are expected to affect both the quantity and the quality of four key Mediterranean products and the whole group of the fruit and vegetables sectors. Two more crops of special interest to the French Mediterranean regions are covered, namely lavender (where varietal conversion is to be assisted) and rice (where financial assistance for new seeds is planned). The four key Mediterranean products are wines, table grapes, dried grapes and olive oil. For wine production the IMPs envisage the reduction of the areas given over to producing table wine and the use of these areas for producing either quality wine (through varietal conversion of vineyards) or a switch to alternative tree crops, primarily nuts (pistachios, walnuts, hazelnuts, almonds) or to fodder and protein crops and exotic fruits. Varietal conversion is also the method to be used to upgrade the quality of table grapes. For dried grapes conversion to other crops particularly nuts is to be assisted financially. Additionally, the IMPs envisage the renewal and the relocation of some of the vineyards for the production of dried grapes away from unsuitable low-lying humid zones.

Production of olive oil is expected to be substantially restructured in many directions. First in both Greece and Italy limited conversion is planned from olive oil production to table olives by concentrating on quality and individuality of the product. Secondly in both these countries conversion to entirely new crops is also to be encouraged and in particular sub-tropical crops, nuts, sunflower and similar protein crops. However, some renovation of oil groves is to be subsidised especially in a few Greek islands and in Mediterranean France. In particular the aim will be to switch to plantations that enable cultural operations to be mechanised. Limited modernisation of olive oil mills is also included among the measures.

Varietal improvement measures are the key policy initiative in the fruit sector where product standardisation will be encouraged by switching to varieties of peaches, apples, pears, cherries, apricots and plums that better meet market requirements. Rationalisation and quality improvement of vegetable production is also planned. All these measures aim at producing product quality without allowing output increases. Crop conversion away from the fruit and vegetable sector will be aimed at encouraging alternative production of aromatic and medicinal plants, seeds and seedlings, subtropical crops, protein and alternative tree crops.

In the forestry sector the measures of Regulation 269/79 are to be extended to better contribute to the preservation of stocks (improved fire prevention methods, creation of nurseries, development of forest exploitation bodies), to the renovation of Aleppo pine, chestnut and cork plantations particularly through the promotion of fast-growing varieties and to the development of parks or wooded areas for extra income from tourism and rearing of game.

The measures for the fisheries sector cover the entire activity including the modernisation of upstream (revictualling, water, ice and fuel supplies) and downstream (unloading, quays, auctions etc.) fishing facilities, the modernisation of the fishing fleet including sponge fishing fleet, development of lagoons for extensive and semi-extensive fishing through infrastructure improvements (dredging, new channels etc.), modernisation of fish (including shell fish) farms and construction of hatcheries for the restocking of lagoons and lakes and for supplying fish farms. However, these measures also aim at maintaining constant the degree of exploitation of the inshore and deep-sea fishing stocks.

An essential part of the IMPs is the financial assistance to increase the market value of products. This involves relatively higher subsidy rates for investment in the processing of agricultural produce into new products and by-products and promotional measures to strengthen the marketing of agricultural products.

Before we look into the external trade implications of the above assistance measures for Mediterranean agriculture, it is important to look at the adjustment measures envisaged for the non-agricultural sector. These measures aim to create jobs with the purpose to offset job losses in agriculture. The methods used to achieve this aim is to encourage (a) the creation or expansion of small and medium sized enterprises and craft industries especially in sectors upstream and downstream of agriculture, (b) rural tourism and (c) the exploitation of renewable energy sources.

Funds earmarked for the non-agricultural sector will be divided approximately on a 50-50 basis for subsidising productive investment and for assisting market developments, management advisory

141

services, infrastructure including the development of small industrial zones and research and development.

In particular, the measures for the development of small and medium sized enterprises (SMEs) are not sectorally tied up but instead are earmarked on a functional basis. Such functionally oriented grants are for the establishment or extension of business advisory services, for improved accessibility to market information (e.g. through sectoral studies), for the improvement of the management and organisational methods, for better access to risk capital, for improving the training of craftsmen, for cooperative ventures in marketing, accounting services etc, for the dismantling, transferring and modifying equipment, for the relocation of workers accompanying firms that move and for start-up aid over a three-year period for bodies responsible for collecting information relating to product and technological innovation and its dissemination. An interesting novelty of the IMPs is assistance to enable the SMEs of the recipient regions to boost their exports to non-EC Mediterranean countries. This is to take place through the availability of grants to cover the cost of travel etc. to seek out partners, expenses associated with exhibitions or demonstrations and the costs of market intelligence required.

To encourage rural tourism aids are made available for the construction or conversion of small hotels, the preparation of farm holiday accommodation, camping and caravaning sites, the establishment of joint agencies for tourism promotion and the restoration of small architectural features of local interest.

4 The IMPs as Adjustment Policy

Adjustment policies aim at lowering the social costs and redistributing the private costs associated with trade-induced changes. In order to attain these objectives without disintegrating into glorified protectionist devices, adjustment policies must fulfil a number of basic criteria (OECD, 1983). More specifically, in order not to impair in the medium-term the efficiency in resource allocation they must :

(a)   be of limited duration
(b)   be attuned to industries, regions or countries that can potentially, and certainly by the time the policy is expected to be terminated, develop comparative advantages,
(c)   make the costs of action as transparent as possible,
(d)   involve public funds jointly with private risk capital,
(e)   be linked to the implementation of particular programmes,

(f)   link assistance with improvements in managerial practices, enrichment of the region's human resources endowment and accessibility to technology.
(g)   remove eventually some of the rigidities impairing the efficiency of market processes from leading to speedy adjustment. In other words they must provide general support for the strengthening of market processes rather than sector specific support.

The IMPs clearly fulfil the first condition. They are multiannual programmes to be terminated after 7 years. However, the Commission's proposals contain the vague promise for a possible second programme after the end of the first seven year period. This may give rise to expectations that can undermine the rationale of the programmes. The third condition is more or less satisfied notwithstanding some difficulties of establishing how far a particular form of spending will actually be designed exclusively for the pursuit of the objectives listed in the IMPs. Conditions (d), (e) and (f) are fulfilled to a considerable extent. Condition (f) is probably the less adequately covered by the programmes mainly because of some vagueness in specifying the skills expected to be developed. If rural tourism is to expand, then training people to acquire the necessary qualifications for running hotels and/or managing farm holiday accommodation appears to be important but gets scarcely any mention in the Commission's programmes. However, it is not difficult to see that conditions (b) and (g) are not fully satisfied by the existing provisions for the IMPs. First, regions were selected for inclusion to the IMPs not necessarily on the basis of the intensity of the expected adjustment problems but because of other considerations motivated by local party political anxieties.

On the basis of its original analysis of the seriousness of the enlargement-induced adjustment problems, the Commission of the EC (1983) selected for inclusion in the IMPs the following areas in France: Languedoc-Rousillon, Corsica, Provence - Côte d'Azur, Aquitaine and Midi Pyrénées; the whole of Greece; and in Italy: the Mezzogiorno, Lazio, Tuscany, Umbria, Marche and Liguria. The major conurbations in all these regions and, in the case of France and Central and Northern Italy, the built-up coastal stretches in which tourism is a year-round activity are excluded from the benefits of the IMPs. When the implementing regulation for the IMPs was approved two years later some interesting additions were made; the departments of Drôme and Ardèche were added to the list of benefiting French regions, whilst to the Italian list the Apennines in Emilia-Romagna and some lagoon areas on the northern Adriatic were added (Commission of the EC, 1985c).

143

Neither the stress for varietal conversions nor the encouragement of new cultivations appears to be based on a clear view of the potential international competitiveness of the proposed varieties or new crops. Can sorghum or maize become internationally competitive in the fields of Sicily or is it really a costly measure of import substitution? Can the production of nuts in Italy, Greece or the Mediterranean regions of France become as competitive as the Californian or Turkish crops? Are labour intensive crops such as table olives (even taking into account the possibilities of quality differentiation) properly attuned to the relative labour cost conditions prevailing in these countries which are continually stressed under the impact of the process of labour earnings convergence working in a highly integrated common market? There is no hard evidence to provide convincing answers to these and similar other questions. The impression is thus given that new products or varietal conversions of existing crops were selected for production support within the IMPs on the basis of a single criterion, i.e. whether they reduce the cost of the CAP. Most of these crops do not come under the market regimes of the CAP and the EC Budget. However, this selection criterion produces different results from the alternative suggested on efficiency grounds, namely relative costs and comparative advantage on the basis of world market prices. Condition (g) is partly fulfilled particularly because expenditure for the IMPs involves compensatory allowances, cessation of farming measures, relocation of activities of the SMEs and the craft industry, back-up measures of agricultural advisory services, technical assistance and infrastructure provision. However the provisions of expenditure directly related to the reduction of the prevailing factor and product market rigidities appear limited. The measures mentioned above as contributing to market rigidity removals represent approximately 44 per cent of all spending under the IMPs. The remaining are selective measures that are sector specific. Sector specific adjustment policy measures produce two opposing effects. If those responsible for the selection of products, industries or regions to be supported forecast well future changes in dynamic comparative advantages the results are efficiency enhancing. Selective, sector or product specific, plans run the danger of encouraging articulated demands for prolonged protection if forecasts go wrong or for continuation of the support beyond what will be regarded optimal from an efficiency viewpoint. The difficulties in monitoring the implementation of sector (or product) specific plans is another issue that must be borne in mind.

5 The IMPs and the trade interests of third countries

Having described the potential impact of the IMPs on the structure of production and having seen some of their limitations regarding their effectiveness in leading to a more efficient resource allocation in the enlarged EC we now proceed to draw the various parts of the analysis together in order to highlight the implications of IMPs on the trade prospects of third countries.

To the extent to which the IMPs will succeed in reducing the volume of production in goods in excess supply in the EC-12 third countries that are producers of similar products can benefit first by hoping to maintain (or expand) their share in the EC imports of traditional products and secondly by facing less price depressing conditions particularly in the residual world market of agricultural produce where the EC disposes of its surpluses. The non-EC Mediterranean countries as producers of the traditional crops whose production in the EC is likely to be rationalised and restructured from the application of the IMPs will be on this count the major beneficiaries. The products whose output is expected to be curtailed through the measures envisaged by the IMPs include table wine, dried grapes, olive oil and fruit and vegetable crops, such as citrus fruit, tomatoes etc. For most cases output reduction in the Mediterranean regions of the EC will reduce domestic, Community, surpluses rather than release market shares for third countries. This is likely to be the case for table wine, olive oil or tomatoes. In these cases the main benefit of third countries engaged in the production of competing crops will come from the improvement in the world market prices following the elimination of the surplus export production of the EC. Countries to experience such marginal benefits are the non-EC Mediterranean countries and for the case of citrus fruit, the United States. The quantitative significance of this reorientation in production is extremely problematic even to guess. The production response of the beneficiaries in the countries receiving support from the IMPs will depend on the exact size of the possibilities of substitution betweeen alternative crops and their attitudes to changes in market uncertainty.

The IMPs by subsidising capital expenditure in agriculture or training and technology in industry are bound to encourage products more intensive in the use of capital (or better quality land in the case of support for expenditure in water supply improvement and irrigation) in agriculture and products more intensive in the use of semi-skilled or skilled labour and intermediate technology in industry.

Elasticities of factor substitution by crop type are hard to find and harder to estimate. In addition another important parameter must be considered. When the producer in response to short-term improvements in the profitability of new types of production enters into new lines he is likely to be faced with a different degree of market uncertainty as far as agricultural products are concerned. The products into which the IMPs try to direct farmers are, with some exceptions for livestock items, non-CAP products. This means that the producer when switching into new lines of production must take into account the fact that the cushioning factor of the CAP will not be there when market disturbances occur. Thus one must be a bit sceptical regarding the ability of programmes such as the IMPs to induce restructuring of production towards non-CAP products when support measures for alternative crops are maintained at levels ensuring satisfactory rates of return. Producer motivation is an imponderable in this exercise.

Assuming restructuring and crop-conversion processes work as envisaged by the IMPs, one would expect a whole list of new varieties, new products or additional products with weak CAP support (e.g. lamb) to be added to Community agricultural output. Table 8.5 provides a basic checklist of the major products whose output is expected to expand following the implementation of the IMPs.

Additional factors may constrain the conversion into new crops. The IMPs increase the maximum rate of aid for processing and marketing for all agricultural products in case of Greece and the Mezzogiorno. Only in the case of the French regions the IMPs specify that the financial assistance for processing and marketing projects must ensure the effectiveness of the structural reform measures for agriculture and fisheries. Furthermore, financial aid for the processing of agricultural products into new products and/or by-products (Regulation 355/77) is made available to new products and by-products irrespective of whether they are listed or not in Annex II of the Treaty of Rome. Now, if the processing operation becomes more attractive it is difficult to see how primary production can be curtailed.

The products included in the list overleaf are indicative. For example, in the structural measures for both Greece and the Mezzogiorno, references are made to the expansion of traditional tree crops to replace traditional vines or olive trees. Furthermore, varietal conversions may have effects similar to that of new products, particularly if they involve types giving rise to early (or late) season production. Table grapes to be marketed in the season 1/11 to 14/7 compete with different groups of producing countries than those marketed for the season 15/7 to 30/10. Varietal conversions may have effects similar to product conversions as far as third country producers are concerned.

Table 8.6: Agricultural Products Favoured by the IMPs

(a)	fodder and protein crops (sorghum, sunflower, maize)
(b)	bovine meat
(c)	lamb and goat meat
(d)	nuts (pistachios, walnuts, hazelnuts, almonds)
(e)	quality wines
(f)	table olives
(g)	products of aromatic and medicinal plants
(h)	wood (pine, chestnut trees)
(i)	cork
(j)	fresh fish and shell fish
(k)	exotic fruit and subtropical vegetables (e.g. avocado)
(l)	seeds

The addition of new crops (and varieties of existing crops) in the agricultural production of the Mediterranean regions of the EC-10 will not necessarily imply a reduction in the market shares of third country producers. First of all, if income elasticities of demand are reasonable, the extra output stimulated by the IMPs could be taken up by expanding demand in the EC. Available data do not provide cause for excessive optimism. As an example, one can take the case of sheepmeat whose production is positively encouraged by the IMPs. Sheepmeat consumption remained almost stagnant in the EC-10 raising only marginally from 969,000 tonnes in 1968 to 972,000 tonnes in 1982. The Commission's rather optimistic forecasts predict consumption at the level of 1,016,000 tonnes for the Ten EC countries (i.e. excluding the Iberian economies) (Green Europe, 1984b). For a few fruit crops (e.g. peaches) estimates of income elasticities of demand are encouraging (Baltas, 1977). In general, one has reasons to worry whether the IMPs are leading towards a market situation where expanding Community production in new products drives out imported varieties because the rate of demand growth falls behind the rate of production expansion stimulated by the IMPs.

For this to happen either of two things must take place. Either, the new products and varieties assisted through financial support from the IMPs become fully competitive and drive out of the European market currently imported products or failing to achieve this, trade measures are introduced to ensure that competitive imports are excluded. The case of sheepmeat can again be used as an example. Since 1980 the EC negotiated voluntary export restraints with 12 countries that agreed to limit their exports to the EC to 319,500 tonnes of carcass equivalent. Such VERs can be adapted downwards if the reconversion encouraged by the IMPs stimulates production that

147

cannot be sustained under the existing trade regime after the termination of these programmes.

There are thus two scenarios one can envisage. Either the financial aid, and the measures of infrastructure, training and technical assistance provided succeed in establishing internationally competitive production in the products listed in table 8.6 in which case third country exports to the EC markets will fall or the measures will not be successful in creating dynamic comparative advantage in which case with the expiry of the seven year period, there will be demands for a further 7-year programme and/or trade measures like VERs to restrict third country suppliers from challenging the slowly moving towards adolescence infant production. In both cases third country producers will be hit.

Table 8.7 provides information that enables us to identify who those vulnerable exporters are likely to be. The table gives the geographical structure of the EC's imports in the unprocessed products where output is encouraged by the IMPs. Obviously, the markets for semi-processed and processed goods derived from the products listed in table 8.6 will also be affected. For example, expansion of sheepfarming will affect not only the market for sheepmeat but also the market for sheep and lamb skin leather, or for sheep and lamb's wool. The growth of sunflower seeds production will also have an impact in the market for sunflower seed oil. Additional local supplies of nuts will affect directly the primary production market but indirectly the roasted nuts market.

Given the information in tables 8.7 and 8.8 one can specify a number of plausible trade outcomes under the assumption of low but positive supply responses to changes in the profitability of alternative types of farming following the implementation of the IMPs.

The share of the USA in the EC markets in fodder and protein crops, almonds, peanuts and other edible nuts, fish, seeds and exotic fruit appears vulnerable to production expansion under the IMPs. On a priori grounds one can argue that the income elasticities of demand do not appear to be pessimistically low to justify making gloomy predictions.

The share of a number of developing economies and particularly Brazil, Argentina, Thailand, India may progressively shrink if the IMPs get successfully under way. More so, will be in the case of Australia (sheepmeat and seeds) and New Zealand (sheepmeat). The significant shares of South Africa and a few other Southern Hemisphere countries in the markets for table grapes or exotic fruit do

148

not suggest any serious adverse effects as their produce comes at a season where EC production is not directly competing with them. In a few markets, e.g. sunflower seeds the export prospects of some Eastern European countries may be affected adversely. From the Mediterranean region, Turkey (almonds, hazelnuts, aromatic and medicinal plants, crustacea and molluscs and seeds), Yugoslavia (bovine meat, aromatic and medicinal plants, crustacea and moluscs and seeds), Cyprus (table grapes), the Maghreb countries (table olives, crustacea and molluscs, fish, almonds, forage products), Egypt (aromatic and medicinal plants) and Israel (forage products, groundnuts, table grapes, exotic fruits and seeds) will be affected marginally given that the relevant demand elasticities are likely to be satisfactory for several of their threatened products.

Excluding the case of nuts where expanding production in the Mediterranean regions of the EC-10 appears to be directly threatening the export interests of the Mediterranean non-EC countries (and to some extent for table grapes) the rest of the policies under the IMPs are leaning towards encouraging production complementarities between the two sides of the Mediterranean basin in accordance with the spirit of the 1982 Memorandum on new initiatives in the EC's Mediterranean Policy (Commission of the EC, 1982a). Trade diversion from expanded production stemming from the IMPs will be primarily against exports from the USA, some Latin American countries and a few Eastern European economies.

An important factor that will ultimately determine whether the ex ante complementarity in production structures between the countries of the two sides of the Mediterranean basin will become effectively promoted depends on the monitoring of the land use patterns in areas subject to additional irrigation, improvements in water systems etc. In the lowland and coastal regions there is a danger of using the newly irrigated areas to increase supplies of products such as vegetables, tomatoes, table grapes etc. rather than the intensive fodder crops favoured by the authors of the IMPs. This danger exists because the relative prices may not change towards the desired direction. The failure has to do with the price setting mechanisms of the CAP. It is thus clear that success of the IMPs depends on progress towards improving the price mechanisms of the CAP and working out towards its reform.

In general of the total expenditure of the IMPs earmarked for the agricultural sector (3,135 million ECU) an amount equal to 51 per cent is spent on measures directly addressed to the reduction of surplus production. The remaining 49 per cent is to be spent on general measures and land improvement schemes that raise productivity for a wide range of alternative types of farming. Their final use will depend

149

Table 8.7: Structure of EC-10 External Imports in Selected Products Favoured by the IMPs

	Value (million ECU)		Share of Major Exporting Regions					
			DMEs	LDCs	CPEs	Mediterranean Non-EC	Spain	Portugal
Forage Products(a)	362.9	*	51.4	43.0	5.1	2.0	6.6	0.3
Soya Beans	3,167.9	**	60.3	39.7	...	...	...	...
Sunflower Seeds	195.2	**	70.4	17.1	11.4	0.7	0.1	...
Bovine meat	644.3	**	39.6	55.9	4.5	11.4	...	...
Meat of sheep and goat	460.6	**	95.1	2.5	2.4	3.7	0.1	...
Almonds	255.6	*	98.2	1.9	...	3.4	21.2	4.2
Groundnuts (peanuts)	339.5	**	56.5	27.7	15.8	4.6	0.6	...
Hazelnuts	231.1	*	99.7	...	...	99.1	...	...
Cashew Nuts	38.4	*	1.3	84.1	14.6	0.5	...	...
Other Edible Nuts(b)	94.9	*	62.4	24.3	3.1	11.6		
Table Grapes	132.0	*	70.8	28.9	0.2	14.7	31.7	...
Table Olives	67.9	***	...	...	...	35.8	55.0	
Aromatic and Medicinal Plants	131.5	**	27.9	55.4	10.7	30.2	2.7	...
Wood of coniferous species (not planned)	2,957.7	**	78.3	1.0	20.7	0.2	0.1	3.7
Cork	23.0	**	92.6	7.4	...	0.9	33.0	58.7
Fish, fresh, chilled or frozen	991.1	*	73.0	23.5	3.5	4.6	7.3	0.9

Table 8.7 (continued)

Products	Value (million ECU)	DMEs	LDCs	CPEs	Mediterranean Non-EC	Spain	Portugal
Crustacea and molluscs	776.8 **	23.3	65.2	5.4	9.9	6.2	0.1
Natural Sponges	3.9 **	17.9	69.2	12.8	76.9	...	...
Avocados, Mangos, Guavas and Mangosteens	121.9 *	26.1	73.7	...	49.2	6.6	...
Seeds	198.1 **	72.9	12.4	14.6	13.4	1.7	0.2

* = 1984   ** = 1985   *** = 1986

(a) = Mangolds, Swedes, Fodder Roots, Hay, Lucerne, products of vegetable origins used for animal food and sweetened forage.

(b) excluding Brazil nuts.

Source: Eurostat, Nimexe series

Table 8.8: Major Third Country Exporters to EC-10 of Products Favoured by the IMPs*

	From the World	From the Mediterranean Region
Forage Products	USA (120.7), Brazil (122.2), Thailand (13.3)	Maghreb (1.8), Yugoslavia (1.5), Israel (1.4)
Soya Beans	USA (1,908.6), Brazil (686.4), Paraguay (82.6)	-
Sunflower seeds	USA (131.8), Argentina (29.7), Bulgaria (6.9), Hungary (15.2)	Turkey (0.044). Israel (0.042)
Bovine meat	Brazil (144.1), Argentina (123.3), Austria (136.4), Uruguay (33.0)	Yugoslavia (73.3)
Meat of sheep and goat	New Zealand (387.7), Australia (31.2), Argentina (10.3)	Yugoslavia (16.9)
Almonds (0.6)	USA (180.7)	Maghreb (0.024)
Groundnuts (peanuts)	USA (181.6), Argentina (56.9), Sudan (2.8)	Maghreb (4.0), Turkey (3.9), Israel
Hazelnuts	India (18.3), Mozambique (3.6), S. Korea (3.3)	Israel (12.7), Turkey (2.3)
Cashew Nuts	USA (48.2), IRAN (10.7), China (9.7)	Turkey (225.2)
Other Edible Nuts	S. Africa (50.4), Chile (12.9)	-
Table Grapes	India (11.0), China (7.6), Secret (34.0)	Israel (0.5)
Aromatic and Medicinal Plants		Cyprus (14.5), Israel (4.2) Yugoslavia (10.6), Egypt (6.8), Turkey (5.2), Israel (0.5)

Table 8.8 (continued)

	From the World	From the Mediterranean Region
Wood of Coniferous species	Efta (ex. Portugal) (1823.7), Canada (236.9), USA (136.6)	-
Cork		- Maghreb (0.31)
Fish, fresh, frozen, chilled	Efta (ex. Portugal) 270.5), USA (118.3), Singapore (22.6), Panama (32.1), Argentina (18.0)	Maghreb (24.8)
Crustaces, Mollusces	Greenland (101.8), India (42.8), Argentina (41.2)	Maghreb (55.6), Turkey (14.9), Yugoslavia (3.3)
Natural Sponges	Japan (0.4), Cuba (0.5)	Tunisia (2.5), Turkey (0.3)
Exotic Fruit	South Africa (14.2), USA (12.2), Mexico (4.5), Brazil (4.2)	Israel (63.4)
Seeds	USA (55.1), Australia (37.2), Japan (8.2)	Israel (5.6), Turkey (13.9), Yugoslavia (3.6)

* For years, notes etc. see previous table. Figures in brackets are in millions of ECU.
Source : Eurostat Nimexe series.

on the appropriate price signals the agricultural policy sends to the farmer. Spanish experience on crop use patterns in newly irrigated land is instructive here (Tovias, 1984). An increase in the irrigated land led to the expansion of the area under cultivation for cereals, industrial crops, citrus fruit and tubers but a shrinkage in the area cultivated for fodder, leguminous plants, fruit other than citrus and olive trees.

A similar danger of disorientation of the programmes exists for their non-agricultural projects. The objectives of the non-agricultural projects are given only in very general terms. The measures are not addressed to specific subsectors but are primarily designed to raise the general level of productivity of the non-agricultural sector (excluding the limited sector specific sums to rural tourism and renewable energy sources). This is a necessary but not a sufficient condition for ensuring that they operate as proper adjustment policies and not as hidden protectionist measures. A sufficient condition is to depoliticise the mechanism of fund distribution among competing claimants. The management of the funds for the IMPs is shared between the European Commission and the Council and as such runs the danger of becoming excessively politicised and torn between efficiency (proper adjustment) objectives and equity considerations. With the institutional set-up adopted by the Council compromise of 25 June 1985, the IMP funds available for the non-agricultural sector may be directed towards helping ailing firms and sectors to survive rather than assisting reconversion of old industries and the nursing of new, dynamic, ones.

Indicative of this danger of disorientation is the set of data in table 8.9 which gives the industrial allocation of the first set of projects financed by the IMPs for non-agricultural development in Greece. More than one third of the first instalment allocated in early 1987 and amounting to about 50 billion drachmas was channelled to the textile and clothing industries. It is difficult to say without more detailed knowledge whether the financial assistance will be used to upmarket the products of the industry or whether it will be used to relieve the ailing industries from pressing financial difficulties or be taken up by labour through wage claims. Only time will show. In the meantime, it is worth noticing that the electronics and data processing sector got just one-tenth of what the textiles and clothing sectors received.

An alternative arrangement that would have provided better guarantees for an efficient use of the funds for the IMPs would have been to place them outside the Commission-Council nexus and move them to the European Investment Bank. These funds would then have been used by the EIB in the context of a new facility entirely managed by the Bank for the purpose of implementing structural adjustment policies

154

(Yannopoulos, 1985). The facility would have been modelled along the lines of the World Bank's Structural Adjustment Facility but with more flexibility. The EIB would then have ensured that finance was to be provided to high interrelated and properly coordinated projects that had the reasonable prospects of standing on their own after the expiry of the IMPs facilities. Banking criteria adapted to the needs for long term financing of integrated projects would then have been used and the danger of politically motivated decisions leading to the degeneration of the programmes into protective devices would have been reduced. The success of an adjustment policy depends thus both on its internal coherence and on the institutional framework used to manage the funds earmarked for the policy. If the IMPs fail to succeed in their objectives, it will be to a considerable extent due to this limitation.

Table 8.9: Sectoral Distribution of the First Greek Submission for Finance of Non-Agricultural Projects from the IMPs, 1987

Sector	Percentage
Textiles and Clothing	35.1
Food and Beverages	21.2
Metals and Metal Manufactures	17.2
Energy	6.7
Ceramics	4.8
Industrial Machinery and Equipment	4.0
Electronics and Data Processing	3.5
Chemicals, Plastics, Pharmaceuticals	2.1
Electrical Apparatuses	1.2
Paper	1.0
Others	3.2

Source : Greek Ministry of Industry

6 Concluding Comments

The IMPs have many characteristics that fulfil the requirements of an efficient anticipatory adjustment policy. But on two counts they present important deficiencies that impair their effectiveness as adjustment measures to trade induced changes. Firstly, the choice of adjustment measures, particularly in the agricultural sector, has been excessively dominated by the need to adapt the agricultural sector of the Mediterranean regions of the EC-10 to the post-enlargement competitive framework on the basis of the principle of minimising the costs of the existing CAP structures rather than on the basis of shifting resources to areas that ensure the competitive survival of the new production in an open world trading system. Some of the crops selected for promotion are distinctly labour intensive which are likely

155

to fit badly within the new relative factor price realities of a highly integrated market. Production stimulated by the measures of the IMPs can then act to divert export trade of competitive world producers. The thrust of this type of trade diversion will be felt by different world regions depending on the particular product. The second drawback is the institutional framework for the management of the funds for the programmes which politicises the whole decision-making process and may eventually lead to the use of IMPs as hidden protectionist devices. The internal coherence of the programmes is not in doubt once one is prepared to accept the objectives of the exercise rather than judge it by the efficiency criteria of positive adjustment policies. Yet even in this field some gaps are too obvious. The IMPs were prepared without much analysis of the types of farmers' response to land improvement measures, attitudes to cooperation, risk aversion etc. They also appear to overestimate the potential for mechanisation given farm structures in Southern Europe.

The IMPs provide only to a limited extent opportunities for encouraging production complementarities between the Southern regions of the Community and the associated Mediterranean countries. In some cases (e.g. production of nuts, table grapes, even aromatic and medicinal plants) they will encourage more competition from within the Community endangering the prospects of competitive exports from the associated countries. Much will depend on how demand for these products within the EC will evolve in relation to the growth of production in the new crops. But also on this, the Commission programmes give the impression of an exercise which is nothing more than a shot in the dark.

Appendix to Chapter 8
Principal Policy Instruments used for the Implementation of the IMPs

Physical Improvement Measures

1. Finance for voluntary reparcelling of land (levelling, improvement of embankments and ditches).
2. Finance for works relating to new irrigation and drainage schemes.
3. Finance for works to protect farmland from erosion and other land improvement schemes provided they are designed for the use of enterprises covered by the programmes.

Sociostructural Measures

4. Compensation to elderly farmers for giving up farmland to younger people (increases in the aid offered through directive 72/160/EEC).
5. Income support for farmers in areas where a certain level of population needs to be maintained (e.g. islands) (increase in the size of allowance under directive 75/268/EEC).

Specific Measures

6. Grants for the improvement of pastures and farm investment (geographical extension of measures of Regulation 1975/82/EEC).
7. Aids for milk testing, genetic improvements of herds and animal health protection.
8. Aids for varietal conversion and restructuring of crop based farms.
9. Finance of pilot projects to increase returns from subtropical crops.
10. Financial schemes to encourage the use of collectively owned machinery for permanent crops.
11. Assistance with the supply of selected seeds, water supplies and mechanisation of production on a group basis.
12. Incentives to keep beef calves on the farms for at least 12 months.
13. Grants for building and improving livestock housing.
14. Relocation and renewal grants for certain crops (mainly vineyards).
15. Grants for restructuring and renovation of certain plantations in the forestry sector.

16. Grants for the development of parks and wooded reserves for game rearing and tourism.
17. Grants for the provision of infrastructure and shore facilities (unloading quays, cold stores etc.) for fishing.
18. Grants for the modernisation of fishing fleets including sponge fleet.
19. Grants for small scale facilities on lakes where substantive fishing takes place and for infrastructure for lagoons and the construction of hatcheries.
20. Increase in the rates of subsidies provided under Regulations 355/77 and 1361/78 for the processing and marketing of agricultural products and extension of their provisions to new products and by-products even for those not covered in Annex II of the Treaty of Rome.

CHAPTER NINE

European Community Trade Options in the New Round of Trade Negotiations

1 Introduction

The strengthening of the GATT rules for the settlement of trade disputes and the extension of existing rules to agricultural trade have been singled out in a previous chapter as possible solutions to the speedy resolution of the trade conflicts with the US generated from the extension of the European customs union. Chapters three to six have shown that a number of trade disputes involving **developing** countries will also be generated by the second enlargement of the EC. This last chapter investigates the possibilities of adapting the GATT framework in both reducing the incidence of such conflicts and in encouraging a speedy resolution to those that are bound to arise in the future.

This chapter explores the alternatives available to the European Community (EC) and argues in favour of the integration of the less developed countries, particularly of their middle income group, into the world trading system. The chapter starts by reviewing the experience of linking trade issues with development cooperation policies especially in the EC and then examines how this experience can be used in deciding on priority areas in the forthcoming multilateral trade negotiations (MTN). The options open to the EC - now the most significant actor in the international trade scene - are finally spelt out.

2 Unfinished Business

Successive post-war MTN and especially the Tokyo Round have succeeded in considerably reducing the level of nominal tariffs applicable on goods imported by industrialised market economies. When the Tokyo Round provisions are finally implemented by 1987 the simple average nominal tariff on imports of semi- and finished manufactures from LDCs will be 5.8% in the EC, and 6.7% in both Japan and the USA whilst trade weighted tariffs on these imports will be 6.7%, 7.7% and 8.7% respectively. When all imports from both LDCs and other regions are taken into account average nominal tariffs are not very much different with the weighted tariff somewhat lower (GATT, 1980 pp. 33-37).

Dispersion of tariffs post-Tokyo will continue to be considerable as will be the extent of tariff escalation. Finished products of export interest to LDCs (e.g. textiles, clothing, footwear, leather, rubber and travel goods) will still be subject to relatively higher tariffs than other categories of finished manufactures. The size of the unfinished business in tariff dismantlement is of course relatively unimportant when compared to the unsettled issues in the area of non-tariff barriers. The rise of 'new protectionism' has been noticeable in both the EC and the rest of the industrialised world.

The Multifibre Arrangement (MFA) from a temporary solution has become a permanent feature of world trade management in clothing and textile products. As the 'new protectionism' takes a variety of covert and obscure forms it is not easy to document correctly the pace of its growth. A recent estimate of the percentage of industrial countries' imports of manufactures covered by non-tariff barriers (NTB) shows that the impact of these barriers does not seem to fall more heavily on imports from LDCs (when compared with imports from industrial market economies). (Table 9.1)

Table 9.1: Percentage of Industrial Countries' Imports of Manufactures subject to NTB

| Importing Area | Imports from: | |
	LDCs	Industrial Market Economies
EC	11.8	15.1
USA	5.5	13.0
Japan	5.4	19.2

Source: World Bank (1984)

Other evidence points out that certain covert forms of NTB, like anti-dumping and anti-subsidy actions, have been affecting more heavily, and indeed increasingly so, imports from LDCc. Of the anti-dumping and anti-subsidy investigations initiated by the Commission of the EC (1984e) during the period 1.1.1981 to 31.12.1983, an increasing proportion was against exporters from LDCs. If we include among the developing countries Romania, China and the countries of Southern Europe then the proportion of investigations involving LDC exporters out of the total number of investigations initiated was as follows:

1981	1982	1983
22.9%	43.1%	52.6%

It is worth noting that these investigations were addressed against products mainly outside the group of textiles, steel and chemicals i.e.

160

against non-traditional manufactures that newly industrialising countries seek desperately to promote.

Despite the general drift of the world towards a more protectionist position, some attempts have been made to improve the market access conditions for LDC exporters. The 1981 GSP arrangements of the EC improved the product coverage of the scheme by including 385 tariff lines of agricultural products and by reducing the number of sensitive groups. Lomé III has marginally liberalised the conditions governing rules of origin. However, only a decisive move towards a new round of MTN can reverse the drift towards the proliferation of the NTB.

3 EC Options

The role of the EC in steering the world towards a new MTN round cannot be underestimated. Whether the EC will respond to the challenge is a matter of considerable political complexity. At the present juncture of the evolution of the EC's external commercial and development cooperation policies, the Community is faced with a distinct choice of whether to consolidate, extend or globalise its present trade regime vis-a-vis the LDCs.

A policy of consolidation will involve the improvement of the existing trade preferences by further tariff cuts or through the broadening of product coverage. The extension option will offer (or improve existing) preferences to regions not currently covered (or less generously treated). The globalisation alternative implies the granting of trade preferences through the global application of general criteria linked to differentiated indicators of development needs. A move towards the globalisation alternative has been made during the introduction of the 1981 GSP by the EC with the shift from global preferential limits to individualised preferential amounts. The result of this change is already apparent with the top 10 beneficiary-supplying countries taking a lower share of the benefits of the scheme.

4 New Protectionism and LDC Export Performance

Despite the unmistakable trend of trade policies to become more protectionist, market penetration growth of LDCs remained faster than total import growth almost throughout the 1970s. The figures in Table 9.2 show that the design of trade policies in the 1970s did not achieve the objective of limiting the increase in import penetration ratios by LDCs.

Even in a group of products where trade is regulated by a panoply of NTB (e.g.the MFA) as is the case of clothing, textiles and footwear,

161

the growth in market penetration ratios by LDC exports has been remarkable.

Table 9.2: Shares in Apparent Consumption : Growth 1970-80

(percentage average annual rates : manufacturing)

	All Imports	Imports from LDCs
EC	4.8	6.7
USA	4.5	8.6
Japan	2.4	5.
OECD	4.3	7.2

Source: H. Hughes and A.O. Krueger (1984).

Table 9.3: Changes in Shares in Apparent Consumption

	EC		USA	
	1970	1980	1970	1980
Clothing	20.6	48.0	6.4	16.3
Textiles	17.4	33.7	4.5	4.4
Footwear	19.7	47.9	13.3	35.7

Source: H. Hughes and A.O. Krueger (1984)

In general the imports to consumption ratio for MFA covered products and hence the growth of penetration of LDC low cost imports had continuously expanded under MFA II throughout the industrialised market economies and was somehow reduced towards the end of the 1970s under MFA II.

This evidence highlights two important issues. The first is the ineffectiveness of trade policy measures, like NTB, that are 'policed' through administrative action rather than through markets. Tariffs are effective policy instruments because their impact works through the markets. NTB are ineffective because their implementation must rely on administrative procedures including administrative discretion - a method both less effective and more costly. Through the linking of issues, bargaining for loopholes, mobilising transnational and transgovernmental allies or simply through cheating, traders subject to NTB can reduce the effectiveness of these measures (Yoffie, 1981). The second fact underlined by the market penetration data in Tables 9.2 and 9.3 is that LDCs with relatively open economies cannot easily be restricted through NTB from increasing their share of industrialised countries' markets. As Hughes and Krueger (1984) argued "it is difficult to imagine that [penetration] rates would have been significantly higher in the absence of any protectionist measures".

Even in the case of trade in agricultural products where EC policies are relatively more protectionist than elsewhere in the industrialised world (with sectoral tariff equivalents of tariff and NTB at 118% for meat, 81% for cereals or 31% for sugar; see N. Kimani, P. Molajoni and T. Mayer, 1984) LDC exports have not performed relatively worse in the EC markets compared to other industrialised countries' markets with less protectionist policy packages. The exercise in Table 9.4 attempts to evaluate LDC performance in agricultural exports by standardising for market growth and relative competitive position (Young, 1972).

Table 9.4: Rate of Change of LDC Exports Compared to Exports of Other Producers (Agricultural Products only)

(average annual rates, 1973-79)		
Exporting Area	Importing Area	
	EC	Other Industrialised Countries
LDCs	30.2	38.7
Other Exporters	26.8	32.2

Source: Commission of the EC (1982b)

Comparing the relative export performance of the two exporting areas to the EC and the other industrial countries, one sees that there is no evidence that LDC agricultural exports to the EC fared comparatively worse there during the period that the CAP was in full application (the overall ratio of the two relative export performance ratios is 1.13/1.20 = 0.94). It is worth recalling however that only 7% of the agricultural exports of the LDCs are subject to levies.

Finally, if from the total agricultural trade of LDCs, one isolates the products for which LDCs are net exporters and which are subject to the CAP rules, then one sees that the proportion of LDC agricultural exports accounted for by such products does not differ greatly whether one considers their exports to the whole world (21%) or their exports to the EC (17%). Thus, the evidence on agricultural trade confirms the finding from the study of market penetration rates for manufacturing imports regarding the ineffectiveness of NTB. (However, the effect on LDCs' real incomes can be different from the direct effect on exports; see Waelbroek and Burniaux, 1985).

163

5 Response to tariff preferences

The discussion so far focused on the response of LDC exporters to the emergence of 'new protectionism' in industrial market economies. Let us now focus on another equally important issue, i.e. the response by LDCs to the availability of tariff preferences and the methods chosen by countries granting preferences, especially the EC, to apply them in practice.

The various tariff preference schemes operated by the EC (GSP, Lomé convention etc.) provide an enabling framework which offers opportunities for export successes. The export supply capability of the beneficiary countries is a crucial factor in determining the extent to which exporters from LDCs can take advantage of these opportunities. Misconceived domestic economic policies in beneficiary countries can easily nullify the advantages of preferential market access to industrialised countries' markets. Looking at aggregate export performance, one may often miss the importance of the enabling framework provided by trade preference schemes. Thus despite the decline in the share of ACP countries in the markets of the EC during the period the Lomé conventions have been in operation, nevertheless notable successes have been recorded by several ACP countries in developing exports of new products to the EC. A high proportion of the ACP countries have started exporting non-traditional exports. Their earnings from these 'new' exports in 1980 were over twice the size of aid disbursement under Lomé I. The number of ACP countries which registered exports of five or more non-traditional manufacturing products between 1975-80 reached 22 out of which eleven states exported 20 or more non-traditional manufactures (Stevens and Weston, 1984).

Again, under the stimulus of Lomé, it appears that the countries which pursued active outwards oriented development strategies have managed to take advantage of the enabling framework provided by the tariff preferences. Similar conclusions can be derived by observing the experience under the EC's GSP, although here Community regulations and member state government actions tend to restrict the market access provisions of the scheme. In 1983, for example, out of total imports of 31 billion ECUs that could possibly be eligible for GSP treatment, only imports of 24 billion ECUs became actually eligible and out of these eligible for GSP imports, only around a third (i.e. 9.3 billion ECUs or 31 per cent) have actually succeeded in securing GSP treatment.

The reasonably satisfactory export performance of LDCs in the face of the rise of new protectionism does not imply that such policies by the industrialised world have at the end no impact on LDCs. Ironically, the result of such measures is to frustrate the efforts of newcomers in manufacturing trade and countries at an early stage of industrialisation. Measures like those contained in the MFA freeze existing trade patterns and deter potential new entrants to the market i.e. the very countries they are purported to help (Das, 1985). Similarly, Voluntary Export Restraints enable already established manufacturing exporters from the developing world to appropriate for themselves the economic rents generated from the application of 'voluntary' quotas. The higher prices that the management of such a quota system gives rise to, induces protected producers in the more developed of the LDCs, i.e. the NICs, to invest in capital intensive production processes and thus outcompete the LDCs at an early stage of industrialisation.

6 Focus on North-South and South-South Trade

Three issues raised in the above discussion are of particular relevance for decisions regarding the agenda of the proposed new round of MTN. The first is the encouraging evidence on the response of LDCs to tariff preferences. The second is the differential response to these preferences and the differences in the ability to overcome NTBs between LDCs pursuing outward development strategies and those following inward looking policies (see additionally A.O. Krueger 1984). The third is the revealed ineffectiveness of 'new protectionism' in actually curtailing the rate of growth of import penetration from LDCs and its undesirable side effect in frustrating the efforts of LDCs at an early stage of industrialisation. Increased awareness of these three issues will eventually help towards the creation of a new climate of opinion facilitating the attempts to bring LDCs directly into the next round of MTN. Furthermore, these findings suggest that North-South trade and South-South trade should become the focus of the new trade talks alongside the other substantive issues of North-North trade and the broadening of the coverage of the GATT system to new fields such as services. Indeed, in view of the resistance to the last initiative, it may be argued that focusing on trade issues by extending the geographical scope of the GATT round could as well have a better chance of success. The potential for trade liberalisation between North and South and among the South may be as great as that among the OECD countries in the 1960s. Integrating the developing countries into the global trading system in a more substantive way will help towards the realisation of this potential and the resumption of faster growth in both North and South. As the data in Table 8.5 show the merchandise imports of three groups of LDCs (i.e. middle income, upper middle income and high income oil exporting) are equivalent to more than 50% of all merchandise imports and imports of manufactures other than machinery and vehicles of the industrial market economies.

165

Table 9.5: World Merchandise Imports : 1982

	(millions of dollars)	
	All Imports	Imports of Manufactures other than machinery and vehicles
Industrial Market Economies	1,212,975	404,325
High Income Oil Exporters	76,211	30,484
Upper Middle Income LDCs	260,541	86,847
Middle Income LDCs	380,209	126,736
Low Income LDCs	56,205	17,375

Source : World Bank (1984)

It is not only in terms of relative size that this trade matters. It is also important in terms of growth potential. The rate of growth of merchandise imports by LDCs since 1973 has been higher than the rate of growth of world trade. The annual rate of growth of the volume of imports into the LDCs was about 8% in 1974-80 compared to 3% for Northern imports. GDP per capita growth rates have also been higher in middle income oil importing LDCs when compared to the corresponding rate of growth of industrial market economies (Table 9.6).

Table 9.6: GDP per Capita Growth : 1960-83

	1960-73	1973-79	1980-83
Industrial Market Economies	3.9	2.1	1.1
Middle Income Oil Importing LDCs	3.8	3.3	1.6
Low Income LDCs	3.0	2.9	5.6

Source : World Bank (1984)

The share of LDCs in total world trade over the last two decades has risen from 20% to 30% and in manufacturing world trade from 6% to 10%. Thus, from the point of view of developed countries' interests, the enhanced integration of LDCs in the world trading system through their structured participation in the new round of MTN makes good sense. Especially for EC trade, LDCs are the Community's largest customer of agricultural products, absorb 43.5% of extra-EC exports of machinery and transport equipment and 26.5% of extra-EC exports of manufactures. Approximately half of extra-EC exports of finished manufactures go to Third World countries.

It makes equally good sense for the LDCs, particularly of the middle income group among them, to take part in the process of liberalising North-South trade on the basis of reciprocity and of extending this process of liberalisation to South-South trade. It is particularly this group of middle income LDCs that stands to gain more from this process of liberalisation. It is worth recalling that between 1965 and 1984 the share of manufactures in the exports of all LDCs to the industrialised market economies rose from 26% to 55% while in the South-South trade it grew from 39% to 62%. Although the share of LDCs in total Northern imports climbed more recently a little down from the 30% level reached in 1980, the share of non-oil LDC exporters rose steadily from 2.9% in 1965 to 5.3% in 1983. It is also of importance for the discussions on the direction of the new round of MTN that the share of total LDC exports destined to each other (South-South trade) increased from 18% in 1965 to 22% in 1980. Since 1970 in particular, trade among LDCs has expanded substantially faster than total world trade, rising from 3.5% of world trade to 7.5%. Analysis of the developments of South-South trade by product groups (UN, 1983) shows that growth was stronger in food and raw materials rather than in manufactures (UN, 1984). Indeed when OPEC countries are excluded from the Southern group, the share of intra-group trade in manufactures remained roughly constant. However, given the fact that the size of the internal markets in LDCs is relatively small, the potential gains from expanded intra-group trade are likely to be large. An accelerated expansion of South-South trade would call for the progressive removal of trade barriers to such trade and for a role in GATT. Progress here has been slow since the preparation of the 1973 protocol of exchange of tariff concessions among LDC signatories. Placing the issue in the broader context of North-South trade liberalisation may step up progress in this area.

LDCs are progressively realising that there are limits as to the extent of non-reciprocal tariff concessions industrial market economies can offer. Emphasis on the mutuality of interests and exchange of tariff concessions on an equitable manner will encourage more decisive moves towards freer trade. In a world of rapidly changing comparative advantages and fast technological change, freer change will ensure a more orderly adjustment of the economies of the LDCs to world market conditions, whilst enabling these countries to obtain modern inputs as cheaply as possible.

167

Thus an alignment of the trade policies of the middle income and upper middle income LDCs to the rules of the international trading regime and the progressive phasing out of the differential treatment in trade will produce distinct gains to these LDCs. It will increase the openness of their economies and remove the anti-export bias of their current tariff structures. The growth record of the.LDCs that have pursued outwards looking strategies is very telling in this respect, when compared with the corresponding record of LDCs with inwards looking trade and development strategies. Secondly, it will offer more opportunities for increasing intra-LDC trade which is likely to be more advantageous to middle income LDCs. Thirdly, it will provide the excuse to governments to curb the power of social groups which receive economic rents from the existing foreign trade regime. It will fourthly, help governments in industrialised market economies to curb the influence of the protectionist lobbies in the North. Fifthly, such a move in trade policies is bound to improve the creditworthiness of LDCs (O'Neil, 1984.) Other gains for LDCs include greater opportunities to exploit economies of scale, the provision of stimuli for increased efficiency in domestic production and for more appropriate exchange rate policies that will set limits to the domestic inflation rate. Also, by enhancing the attraction of low wage locations freer North-South trade will encourage more foreign direct investment to LDCs. Discussions about integration of groups of LDCs in the world trading system raise inevitably the thorny issue of graduation and the accompanying adjustment costs. There is no shortage of proposals here regarding the financing of industrial readaptation required to adjust to external competitive pressures. Frank (1979) has proposed the setting up of a capital fund within the World Bank out of which project loans for industrial readaptation could be made available to those LDCs willing to expose their industries to international competitive pressures. The European Investment Bank can play a similar role for the EC (Yannopoulos, 1985). Alternatively, Hufbauer and Schott (1985) propose the conversion of existing import quotas to tariffs and the use of the resources raised to finance industry adjustment. This incentive scheme could operate both in the North and in the South.

Recent econometric modelling of the effects on LDCs from trade liberalisation worldwide (Whalley, 1984) suggests that simultaneous trade liberalisation in both North and South will increase world welfare but would redistribute income, through terms of trade changes, from LDCs to industrialised countries. However, this analysis is of limited relevance for trade liberalisation decisions because it ignores the effect on welfare and income distribution from the removal of NTB and the associated rent seeking activities.

7 Agenda Suggestions for the 8th GATT Round

The main thrust in the arguments advanced in this chapter can be summarised as follows :

(a)   The proliferation of NTB has not achieved the objective of reducing import penetration from LDCs into industrialised countries' markets whilst it produced adverse side effects for new starters in the developing world.

(b)   The granting of non-reciprocal tariff preferences did produce results for a group of LDCs that operated more outwards looking trade and development strategies.

(c)   There are strong indications that the potential for the expansion of North-South and South-South trade is substantial and could provide a stimulus to further growth for both the LDCs and the industrialised countries.

(d)   Further expansion of Southern exports to the North cannot take place only on the basis of additional trade preferences in the North. It requires additional increased trade openness of the Southern countries.

Thus dismantling of tariffs and NTB simultaneously on both sides with appropriate institutional arrangements to face the inevitable adjustment costs will produce beneficial results on both sides and particularly on the middle income LDCs. The package of measures that would make feasible the gains from trade liberalisation could, indicatively, include :
(i)   A commitment to phase out over a 5-10 year period the MFA and various hidden subsidies to the protected industries in the North. Similar commitments to be also undertaken in other areas of managed trade.
(ii)   Reform of the procedures of article 19 of the GATT with the replacement of GATT panels with multilateral surveillance.
(iii)   Reciprocal commitments on the part of the middle income LDCs to liberalise their trading regimes at a pace which will take account of their period of insulation from the world economy.
(iv)   Adjustment assistance policies for both the Northern and the Southern states along the lines suggested by Frank (1979) and Hufbauer and Schott (1985).

The Commission of EC could take the lead in these matters by putting forward such proposals. In this way the present impasse stands a better chance to be bypassed whilst the Community will achieve the long overdue intregration of its trade and development cooperation policies. Opposing this policy option on the grounds that it cannot be pursued in a Third World ridden with heavy debts, misses entirely the point. Only in a growing world economy can the debt problems of the LDCs be solved.

BIBLIOGRAPHY

Aitken, N.D. (1973), The effects of EEC and EFTA on European Trade: a temporal cross section analysis, *American Economic Review*, vol. 68.

Aktan, O.H. (1985), The Second Enlargement of the European Communities : probable effects on the members and new entrants, *European Economic Review*, vol. 28, pp 279-308.

Ashoff, G. (1982) Consequences of Southward Enlargement for EC-Latin American Relations, *Intereconomics*, September-October, pp 225-233.

Axelrod, R. (1981), The Emergence of Cooperation Amongst Egoists, *American Political Science Review* vol. 75, pp 306-318.

Balassa, B. (1965), Trade liberalisation and "revealed" comparative advantage, *The Manchester School*, vol. 33, pp 99-123.

Balassa, B. (1967) Trade creation and trade diversion in the European Common Market, *The Economic Journal*, March.

Balassa, B. (1975), *European Economic Integration* , North Holland Publishing Company.

Balassa, B. (1984), International Trade in Manufacturing Goods and Structural Changes in Industrial Countries, *World Bank Staff Working Paper*, No. 611.

Balassa, B and C. (1984), Industrial Protection in the Developed Countries,*The World Economy*, vol. 7, No. 2, June, pp 179-196.

Baldwin, R.E. & T. Scott Thompson (1984), Responding to Trade-Distorting Policies of Other Countries, *American Economic Review*, vol. 74, No. 2, May, pp 271-276.

Baltas, N. (1977), *The Role of State Intervention in Fruit Production*, Research Department, Agricultural Bank of Greece, Study No. 1, Athens (in Greek).

Bardhan, P.K. (1970), *Economic Growth, Development and Foreign Trade,* John Wiley, New York.

Beissner, K.H. and H.R. Hemmer, (1981), The Impact of the EC's Agricultural Policy on its Trade with Developing Countries, *Intereconomics*, March/April, pp 55-60.

Benyon, F. and J. Bourgeois (1984), The European Community - United States Steel Arrangement, *Common Market Law Review*, vol. 21, June, pp 305-354.

Bondy, B. (1983), Protectionism : Challenge of the Eighties, Union Bank of Switzerland, *Studies on Business, Banking and Monetary Topics*, No. 88, Zurich.

Brada, J.C. and L.J. Wipf (1976), Romanian Exports to Western Markets, in J.C. Brada (ed.), *Quantitative and Analytical Studies in East-West Economic Relations*, Studies in East European and

171

Soviet Planning Development and Trade, No. 24, Indiana University, Bloomington, USA.

Braun, J.V. and H. Hartwig (1982), Egypt and the Enlargement of the EEC : Impact on the Agricultural Sector, *Food Policy* , vol. 7, No. 1, February, pp 46-56.

Brecher, R.A. (1974), Optimum Commercial Policy for a Minimum Wage Economy, *Journal of International Economics*, May.

Britton, A. (1983), *The External Constraint on Growth*, mimeographed.

Bulletin (1980), *UN Economic Bulletin for Europe,* vol. 32, pp 80-81.

Caves, R.E. (1976), Economic Models of Political Choice : Canada's Tariff Structure, *Canadian Journal of Economics*, vol. 9, No. 2, pp 278-300.

Caves, R.E. and R.W.Jones (1973), *World Trade and Payments : An Introduction*, Little, Brown and Company, Boston, pp 271-273.

Cline, W.R. (1983), "Reciprocity": A New Approach to World Trade Policy?, in R.C.Cline (ed.), *Trade Policy in the 1980s*, MIT Press, pp 121-158.

Commission of the EC (1976), Opinion to the Council on the Greek application for accession, *Bulletin of the EC*, Supplement, 5/76.

Commission of the EC (1978a), Opinion to the Council on Portuguese application for accession, *Bulletin of the EC*, Supplement, 5/78.

Commission of the EC (1978b), Opinion to the Council on Spain's application for accession, *Bulletin of the EC*, Supplement, 9/78.

Commission of the EC (1978c), *The Customs Union: Today and Tomorrow,* Record of the conference held in Brussels on 6,7 and 8 December 1977.

Commission of the EC (1981a), L'élargissement de la Communauté Européenne : *L'Impact de l'Adhésion de l'Espagne sur certains régions Francaises, notamment ses régions frontières continentales,* Internal Documentation on Community Regional Policy, No. 12, October, Brussels.

Commission of the EC (1981b), *Répercussions de l'élargissement de la CEE sur les régions Italiennes*, Internal Documentation on Community Regional Policy, No. 13, October, Brussels.

Commission of the EC (1982a), Communication Regarding Overall Mediterranean Policy in an Enlarged EC, *COM (82)353*, 24 June, Brussels.

Commission of the EC (1982b), The CAP and the EC's trade relations in the agricultural sector, *SEC (82) 1223*, 14 July, Brussels.

Commission of the EC (1983), The Commission's proposals for the Integrated Mediterranean Programmes, *COM (83) 24 final*, 23 March, Brussels.

Commission of the EC (1984a), Recommendation for a Council Decision on the simplification and harmonisation of customs procedures, *COM (84) 617 final*, 13 November, Brussels.

Commission of the EC (1984b), Proposal for a Council Decision authorising extension or tacit renewal of certain trade agreements concluded between member states and third countries, *COM(84/) 579 final*, 20 October, Brussels.

Commission of the EC (1984c), Communication from the Commission to the Council : Request for consultation on bilateral agreements between member states and third countries, *COM(84) 651 final*, 26 November, Brussels.

Commission of the EC (1984d), Annual Economic Report, Brussels, *COM(84) 587 final*, 29 October, Brussels.

Commission of the EC (1984e), Second Annual Report of the Community's anti-dumping and anti-subsidy activities, *COM(84) 721 final*, 17 December, Brussels.

Commission of the EC (1984f), *The Regions of Europe*, Second Periodic Report on the Social and Economic Situation and Development of the Regions of the Community, COM(84) 40 final/2, Brussels.

Commission of the EC (1985a), Proposal for a Council Regulation (EEC) on the entry in the accounts and terms of payment of the amounts of import duties or export duties resulting from a customs debt, *COM (84) 739 final*, 7 January, Brussels.

Commission of the EC (1985b), Perspective for the Common Agricultural Policy: The Green Paper of the Commission, *COM(35) 333 final*.

Commission of the EC (1985c), Proposal for a Council Regulation, instituting the Integrated Mediterranean Programmes, *Official Journal*, OJC179, 17 July, Brussels.

Cooper, C.A. and B.F. Massell (1965), Toward a General Theory of Customs Union for Developing Countries, *Journal of Political Economy*, 73, October, pp 461-476.

Corden, W.H. (1986), Policies Towards Market Disturbance, in R.H. Snape (ed.), *Issues in World Trade Policy: GATT at the Crossroads*, Hamilton, pp 121-139.

Cripps, F. (1983), Britain Europe and Macroeconomic Policy, in R. Jenkins (ed.), *Britain and the EEC*, Macmillan, pp 111-130.

Daniel, P. (1984), Interpreting Mutual Interest : Non-fuel Minerals in EEC and ACP relations, in C. Stevens (ed.), *EEC and the Third World : A Survey (4)*, Hodder and Stoughton, pp 63-88.

Das, D.K. (1985), Dismantling the Multifibre Arrangement, *Journal of World Trade Law*, vol. 19, No. 1, January-February.

173

Dominick, M.F. (1984), Countervailing State Aids to Steel : A case for international consensus, *Common Market Law Review*, vol 21, January, pp 355-403.

Donges, J.B. (1976), The Economic Integration of Spain with the EEC : problems and prospects, in A. Shlaim and G.N. Yannopoulos (ed.), *The EEC and the Mediterranean Countries*, Cambridge University Press.

Donges, J. et al, (1982), *The Second Enlargement of the European Community - Adjustment Requirements and Challenges for Policy Reform.* Tübingen: J.C.B. Mohr (for the Kiel Institute of World Economics).

Donges, J and K.W. Schatz (1980), Competitiveness and Growth Prospects in an Enlarged European Community, *The World Economy*, pp 213-228.

Donges, J and K.W. Schatz (1985), Portugal and Spain entering the Common Market - Their Industrial Competitiveness Revisited. *Kiel Working Papers No. 233*, Kiel Institute of World Economics.

Duchêne, F. (1985), *The European Community and the Mediterranean*, European Documentation, Periodicals 3-4, Brussels.

ECLA (1981), *Las relaciones económicas entre España e Iberoamérica*, United Nations Commission for Latin America, Santiago de Chile.

Eichengreen, B.J. (1983), Protection, Real Wage Resistance and Employment, *Weltwirtschaftliches Archiv*, vol. 119, No. 3, pp 729-751.

El-Agraa, A.M. (1980a), Measuring the Impact of Economic Integration, in A.M. El-Agraa (ed.), *The Economics of the European Community*, Philip Allan, pp 95-110.

El-Agraa, A.M. (1980b), The Common Agricultural Policy, in A.M. El-Agraa (ed.), op. cit, pp 134-158.

European Economy (1984), *Opinion to the Council and the Commission on the Issue of Protectionism*, Economic Policy Committee, No. 19, March, pp 131-132.

FAO (1979), *Commodity Review and Outlook 1979-80*, FAO Economic and Development Series, No. 17, Rome.53.

Fauvel, L. (1971), The Common Agricultural Policy of the European Economic Community and North American Exports, in C. Kindleberger and A. Shonfield (eds), *North American and Western European Economic Policies*, Macmillan, London, pp 298-320.

Fennel, R. (1980), *The Common Agricultural Policy of the European Community*, Granada, London.

Finger, J.M and M.E. Kreinin (1979), A Measure of Export Similarity and its Possible Uses, *The Economic Journal* , pp 905-912.

Frank, I. (1979), The Graduation Issue of LDCs, *Journal of World Trade Law*, vol. 13, July-August.

Gaines, D.B., W.E. Sawyer and R. Sprinkle (1981), EEC Mediterranean Policy and US Trade in Citrus, *Journal of World Trade Law*, vol. 15, No. 5, September-October, pp 431-439.

Gard, L.M. and J. Riedel (1981), Safeguard Protection in Developed Countries : Assessment of the Implications for Developing Countries, *Weltwirtschaftliches Archiv,* vol. 116, No. 1, pp 471-491.

GATT (1980) *Supplementary Report by the Director General of the GATT* on the Tokyo Round of Multilateral Trade Negotiations, Geneva.

Goldstein, J.L. and S.D.Krasner (1984), Unfair Trade Practices : The Case for a Differential Response, *American Economic Review*, vol. 74, No. 2, May, pp 282-287.

Green Europe (1984a), *Agriculture in the United States and in the European Community : A Comparison*, Agricultural Information Service of the Directorate General for Information, European Community, No. 200, Brussels.

Green Europe (1984b), *Sheepmeat,* No. 201, May, Brussels.

Green Europe (1986), *A Future for Community Agriculture : Community Guidelines*, Newsflash, No. 34, Brussels.

Gutmann, E. (ed.) (1984), *Israel and the Second Enlargement of the European Community : Political and Economic Aspects*, The European Research Centre, The Hebrew University of Jerusalem.

Hamilton, C. (1986), Restrictiveness and International Transmission of the "New" Protectionism, *Seminar Paper No. 367*, Institute for International Economic Studies, University of Stockholm.

Harris, S. et al. (1978), *The Renegotiation of the ACP-EEC Convention of Lomé with special reference to agricultural products*, Commonwealth Secretariat, London.

Harris, S., A. Swinbank and G. Wilkinson (1984), *The Food and Farm Policies of the European Community* , John Wiley & Sons, Chichester.

Hewett, E.A. (1976), A gravity model of CMEA trade, in J.C. Brada (ed), op. cit. pp 1-16.

Hewitt, A. (1982), EEC policies towards the least developed: an analysis, in C. Stevens (ed.) *EEC and the Third World : A Survey (2)*, Hodder and Stoughton, pp 125-136.

Hine, R.C. (1985), *The Political Economy of European Trade : An Introduction to the Trade Policies of the EEC*, Wheatsheaf Books, Brighton, Sussex.

175

Hirschman, A.O. (1945), *National Power and the Structure of Foreign Trade*, University of California Press.

Hufbauer, G.C. (1983), Subsidy Issues After the Tokyo Round, in W.R. Cline (ed.), *Trade Policy in the 1980s*, MIT Press, pp 327-361.

Hufbauer, G.G. and Schott, J.J. (1985) *Trading for Growth : The Next Round of Trade Negotiations*, Institute for International Economics, Washington.

Hughes, H. and Krueger, A.O. (1984), Effects of Protection in Developed Countries on Developing Countries' Exports of Manufactures, in R.E.Baldwin and A.O. Krueger (eds), *The structure and evolution of US trade policy*, Chicago University Press, (Chapter 11).

Hughes, H. (1986), The Political Economy of Protection in Eleven Industrial Countries in R.H. Snape (ed), *Issues in World Trade Policy : GATT at the Crossroads*, Macmillan, London, pp 222-237.

Jackson, J.H. (1978), The Crumbling Institutions of the Liberal Trade System, *Journal of World Trade Law*, vol. 12, No. 93, March-April.

Jackson, J.H. (1983), GATT Machinery and the Tokyo Round Agreements, in W.R. Cline (ed.), *Trade Policy in the 1980s*, MIT Press, pp 159-187.

Johnson, H.G. (1954), Optimal Tariffs and Retaliation, *Review of Economics and Statistics*, vol. 21, No. 2, pp 142-153.

Johnson, H.G. (1965), An Economic Theory of Protectionism, Tariff Bargaining, and the Formation of Customs Unions, *Journal of Political Economy*, vol. LXXIII, June.

Johnson, H.G. (1967), Trade Preferences for Manufactured Goods, in *Economic Policies Towards Less Developed Countries*, Allen and Unwin, London.

Josling, T.E. (1979), The European Community Agricultural Policies and the Trade Interests of the Developing Countries, *ODI Review*, 1.

Josling, T.E. (1980a), *Developed Country Agricultural Policies and Developing Countries Supplies : The Case of Wheat*, International Food Policy Research Institute, Washington.

Josling, T.E. (1980b), Questions for Farm Policy in an Enlarged European Community, *The World Economy*, pp 343-61.

Kebschull, D. (1976), The effects of EEC preferences to associated states on trade flows, in A. Shlaim and G.N. Yannopoulos (eds), *The EEC and the Mediterranean Countries*, Cambridge University Press, London, pp 53-71.

Kellman, M, and T. Schroder (1983), The export similarity index : some Structural Tests, *Economic Journal*, vol. 93, March, pp 193-198.

176

Kierzkowski, H. (ed.) (1984), *Monopolistic Competition in International Trade*, Oxford University Press.

Kimani, N., Molajoni, P. and Mayer, T. (1984), Effects of Increased Market Access on Exports of Developing Countries, *IMF Staff Papers*, December.

Kirschke, P. (1981), Wohlfahrtsökonomische Konsequenzen der gemeitsamen Agrarpreisspolitik in einer erweiterter EG, *Schriften der Geselschaft für Wirtschafts und Sozialwissenschaften des Landbanes*, Vol. 18, pp 421-442.

Kreinin, M.E.(1972), Effects of the EEC on imports of manufactures, *The Economic Journal*, vol. 82.

Kreinin, M.E. (1973), The static effects of EEC enlargement on trade flows, *Southern Economic Journal*, April.

Kreinin, M.E. (1974), *Trade Relations of the EEC: an empirical investigation*, Praeger, New York.

Kreinin, M.E. (1976), US Trade Interests and the EEC Mediterranean Policy, in A. Shlaim and G.N. Yannopoulos (ed.), op. cit. pp 33-52.

Krueger, A.O. (1984), Trade Policies in Developing Countries, in R.W. Jones and P.B. Kenen (eds), *Handbook of International Economics*, vol. 1, pp. 519-569.

Lal, D. (1979), Comment on Nield, in R. Major (ed.), *Britain's Trade and Exchange Rate Policy*, NIESR, Economic Policy Papers 3, Heinemann Educational Books, pp 24-36.

Machlup, F. (1977), *A History of Thought on Economic Integration*, Macmillan, London.

Marrese, M. and J. Vanous (1983), Unconventional Gains from Trade, *Journal of Comparative Economics*, vol. 7, pp 382-399.

Marsh, J. (1978), The Impact of the enlargement on the Common Agricultural Policy, in Wallace (ed.), *A Community of Twelve?* , Bruges, pp 179-210.

Mayes, D.G.(1978), The Effects of Economic Integration on Trade, *Journal of Common Market Studies*, vol. 17, No. 1.

McCulloch, R. and J. Pinera (1977), Trade as Aid: The Political Economy of Tariff Preferences for Developing Countries, *The American Economic Review*, December, pp 959-967.

McQueen, M. and R. Read (1986a), The Effects of Portugal's accession to the European Community on the exports of ACP countries, *Estudos de Economia*, vol. 6, No. 3, pp 369-384.

McQueen, M. and R. Read (1986b), Prospects for the exports of the ACP countries in a Community of Twelve, *University of Reading Discussion Papers in European and International Social Science Research*, No. 13 July.

Meat and Livestock Commission, (1978), Greece, Portugal and Spain in the EEC? *International Market Survey*, Winter Issue.

Mishalani, P. et al. (1981), The pyramid of privilege, in *C. Stevens (ed.), EEC and the Third World : A Survey-1* , London, Hodder and Stoughton, pp 60-82.

Noelke, M. and R. Taylor (1982), *EEC Protectionism : Present Practice and Future Trends*, European Research Associates, Brussels.

OECD (1983), *Positive Adjustment Policies*, Paris.

O'Neil, H. (1984) HICs, MICs, NICs, and LICs: Some Elements in the Political Economy of Graduation and Differentiation, *World Development*, vol. 12, pp 693-712.

Paarlberg, R.L. (1986), Responding to the CAP: Alternative strategies for the USA, *Food Policy*, May pp 157-173.

Pasca, R. (1978), Mediterranean agricultural trade problems and the effects of the EC policies, *European Review of Agricultural Economics*, vol. 5, 3/4.

Patterson, E. (1984), Features of the Omnibus Trade Act in the United States, *The World Economy*, vol. 7, No. 4, December, pp 407-420.

Pearce, J. (1983), Export Credit : The Implications of the 1982 Revision for Developing Countries, in C. Stevens (ed.), *EEC and the Third World : A Survey (3)*, Hodder and Stoughton, pp 53-63.

Pepelasis, A. et al, (1980), *The Tenth Member-Economic Aspects,* Mediterranean Challenge, IV, Sussex European Studies, No. 7, Brighton.

Pinder, J. (1973), The Community and the Developing Countries : Associates and Outsiders, *Journal of Common Market Studies*, vol. 12, pp 53-77.

Pomfret, R. (1981), The Impact of the EEC enlargement on non-member Mediterranean countries' exports to the EEC, *Economic Journal*, vol. 91, September pp 726-730.

Pomfret, R. (1985), The Trade Diversion due to EC Enlargement : A Comment on Sawyer's Estimate, *Weltwirtschaftliches Archiv.* vol. 121, No. 3, pp 560-563.

Robertson, D. (1969), Trade Liberalisation and the European Trade Blocks, in G.R.Denton (ed.), *Economic Integration in Europe*, Weidenfeld and Nicolson, pp 55-82.

Robertson, D. (1976), The European Community's Mediterranean Policy in a World Context, in A. Shlaim and G.N. Yannopoulos (eds), op. cit. pp 325-348.

Robson, P. (1984), *The Economics of International Integration*, Allen and Unwin, second edition.

Roemer, J.E. (1977), The effect of sphere of influence and economic distance on the commodity composition of trade in manufactures, *Review of Economics and Statistics,* pp 318-327.

Rollo, J.M.C.(1979). The second enlargement of the European Economic Community - Some Economic Implications with special reference to agriculture, *Journal of Agricultural Economics*, Vol. XXX, September.

Sampson, G.P. and A.J.Yeats (1979). An Evaluation of the Common Agricultural Policy as a Barrier Facing Agricultural Products in the EEC, *American Journal of Agricultural Economics*, February, pp. 96-106.

Sawyer, G.W. (1984), The Effects of the Second Enlargement of the EC on US exports to Europe,*Weltwirtschaftliches Archiv*, vol. 120, No. 3, pp 572-579.

Sellekaerts, W. (1971), The effects of the EEC on her members' imports from the communist countries of Eastern Europe, *Southern Economic Journal*, January, vol. 37, No. 3, pp 323-333.

Sellekaerts, W. (1973), How meaningful are empirical studies on trade creation and diversion? *Weltwirtschaftliches Archiv*, vol. 109, pp 519-551.

Shaked, A. and J. Sutton (1984), Natural, Oligopolies and International Trade, in *H. Kirerzkowski (ed.)*, op. cit.

Shepard, L. (1986), Cartelisation of the California-Arizona Orange Industry, 1934-1981, *Journal of Law and Economics*, vol. 29, April, pp 83-123.

Shlaim, A. and G.N. Yannopoulos (1976), *The EEC and the Mediterranean Countries*, Cambridge University Press, London.

Smith, M. (1983), *Trade Relations between the European Community and the United States : Common Course or Divergent Paths?*, UACES Proceedings 3, London.

Stevens, C. and Weston, A. (1984), Trade Diversification : Has Lomé helped? in C. Stevens (ed.) *EEC and Third World*, A Survey, 4. Hodder and Stoughton, London.

Sutton, J. (1984), Towards a Protectionist Europe/A preliminary draft, *The Royal Institute of International Affairs*, (mimeographed).

Tangermann, S. (1984), *US Farm Policy Options and EC Response*, American Enterprise Institute Occasional Papers.

Thorbecke, E. and H. Pagoulatos (1975), The effects of European economic integration on agriculture, in B. Balassa (1975), *op. cit.* (chapter 8).

Tinbergen, J. (1960), The Impact of the European Economic Community on Third Countries, *Reprint Series*, No. 11, College of Europe, Bruges.

Tovias, A. (1977), *Tariff Preferences in Mediterranean Diplomacy*, Macmillan for Trade Policy Research Centre, London.

Tovias, A. (1979a), The Outcome of Closer Economic Links with EEC for LDCs' exports previously dumped in world markets: an empirical investigation, *Oxford Economic Papers*, vol. 31, March, No. 4.

Tovias, A. (1979b), EEC Enlargement - The Southern Neighbours, The *Mediterranean Challenge - III*, Sussex European Papers, No. 5, Brighton.

Tovias, A. (1984), The Effects of the Second Enlargement of the European Community upon Israel's Economy, in E. Gutmann (ed), *op cit.*

Tovias, A. (1986), *L'Impact du Nouvel Enlargissement des Communautés Européennes sur ses Relations avec les Etats-Unis,* mimeographed.

Truman, E.M. (1969), The European Economic Community : trade creation and trade diversion, *Yale Economic Essays*, Spring issue.

United Nations (1983), Recent Experiences in Economic Cooperation among Developing Countries and Possibilities for Progress in the 1980s, *Supplement to World Economic Survey*, Dept. of International Economic and Social Affairs, New York, pp. 1-20. Also, the follow-up in the 1984 *Supplement*, pp 14-20.

United Nations (1984), Structural Changes and North-South Trade, with Emphasis on the Trade of the ECE Region, 1965-1983, *Economic Bulletin for Europe*, vol. 36, No. 4, pp 481-515.

Waelbroek, J. and J.M. Burniaux (1985), The Impact of the CAP on the Developing Countries : A General Equilibrium Analysis, in C. Stevens and J. Veloren van Themaat (eds) Pressure Groups, Policies and Development, *EEC and the Third World : A Survey 5*, Hodder and Stoughton, London, pp 123-140.

Wall, D. (1983), Britain, the EEC and the Third World, in R. Jenkins (ed.), *Britain and the EEC*, Macmillan, London, pp 178-206.

Wallace, W. (1982), Europe vis-a-vis the leading economic powers, in J.A. Girão (ed.), *Southern Europe and the Enlargement of the EEC*, Economia, Lisbon, pp 109-125.

Weintraub, S. (1985), Selective Trade Liberalisation and Restriction in E.H. Preeg (ed.), *Hard Bargaining Ahead : US Trade Policy and Developing Countries*, Transaction Books, New Brunswick (USA).

Wellenstein, E. (1986), Political Implications of US-EC Economic Conflicts (1) - Euro-American Turbulence: The Trade Issue, *Government and Opposition*, vol. 21, No. 4, pp 387-395.

Whalley, J. (1984), *Trade Liberalisation Among Major World Trading Areas*, The MIT Press, Cambridge, Mass.

Wolf, M. (1983), The European Community's Trade Policy, in R. Jenkins (ed.), Britain and the EEC, Macmillan, London, pp. 151-177.

180

World Bank (1984), *World Development Report*, Oxford, University Press.

Yannopoulos, G.N. (1980), Sensitivity of industrial sectors to Common Market competition, in *The Tenth Member - economic aspects*, Mediterranean challenge - IV, Sussex European Studies, No. 7.

Yannopoulos, G.N. (1985), Integration and Convergence : Lessons From Greece's Experience in the European Community, *Intereconomics*, vol. 20, No. 2, March-April, pp 93-97.

Yoffie, D.B.(1981) The Newly Industrialising Countries and the Political Economy of Protectionism, *International Studies Quarterly*, vol. 25, No. 4, pp 569-599.

Young, C. (1972) Association with the EEC : Economic Aspects of the Trade Relationship, *Journal of Common Market Studies*, Vol. 11, December, pp 120-135.

138,140,143,146

Japan : 18,19,25,46
Jordan : 64,81

Latin America : 2,56,62,
    91,99,103,109-110,
    149
Lebanon : 64,81
Lesotho : 58
Libya : 2
Lomé countries : 2,5,9,22,
55,161,164
Luxembourg : 89

Maghreb countries : 45,85,
    86,95,149
Malta : 3,45,81,82,95,107
Mashrek countries : 3,95
Mediterranean countries :
    2,3-5,12,44,45,53-55,
    64,67-70,81-93,96-
    102, 114,130,
    131,145,149, 156
Mediterranean policy :
    9,21,92,93,95,96,114,
    115,120,149
Morocco : 54,64,81,101,
    106
Most Favoured Nation:
    1,20,46,82
Multifibre Arrangement :
    2,3,20,25,160,162,

Multilateral Trade
Negotiations : 18,23,26,
    57,126,159,167

Natural Oligopolies : 16
Netherlands : 122
New Zealand : 2,5,46,148
NICs : 19,38,165
Non-associated LDCs :
    2,31,62
Non-European DMEs :

Non-tariff Barriers :
    35,44,82,83,86-90,
    96,109,117,160,

North-South trade : 165-
    169
Norway : 4

OECD : 1,17,99,142
OPEC : 167
optimum tariffs : 16
outward processing : 18

Pacific basin : 112
Portugal : 3,4,8,9,40,42,
    45,49,56,60-62,64,71,
    81-92,107,111,

Preference erosion :
    6,40,44-52,56,63,
    65,68-71,88-90,96,
    100,103
Preference margins :

Protectionism : 1,15-
    17,24,25,58,126,130,
    155,161,164,

Reciprocity : 20,82,114,
    169
Retaliation : 15,23,115,
    116,119-125,127
Revealed Comparative
Advantage : 10,41,47,
    90,134
Romania : 2,28,32,
    25,46,160
Rules of origin : 89

Safeguards : 19,22,62
Sensitive Products :

Similarity of trade : 64,

Somalia : 58
South Africa : 46,148
South-East Asia : 2,91,99
Southern Europe : 34,47,
    57,63,88,103,156,160
Spain : 3,4,8,9,13,40,42,
    45,56,60-62,64,71,
    122,130,134, 136,154
STABEX : 70

183